EARLY DAYS, EARLY DANCERS

EARLY YEARS OF THE NATIONAL BALLET OF CANADA

D1593943

JOCELYN TERELL ALLEN

INANNA
F.A.R. Art Series

Published in Canada by
Inanna Publications and Education Inc.
210 Founders College, York University
4700 Keele Street, Toronto, Ontario M3J 1P3
Telephone: (416) 736-5356 Fax (416) 736-5765
Email: inanna.publications@inanna.ca Website: www.inanna.ca

We gratefully acknowledge the support of the Canada Council for the Arts and the Ontario Arts Council for our publishing program. We also acknowledge the financial support of the Government of Canada.

Printed and Bound in Canada.

Cover photograph: Jocelyn Terell with Hans Meister and Patrick Hurde, publicity shot for *One in Five*. Courtesy of the National Ballet Archives.

Cover design: Val Fullard

Library and Archives Canada Cataloguing in Publication

Title: Early days, early dancers : early years of the National Ballet of Canada / Jocelyn Terell Allen.
Names: Allen, Jocelyn Terell, 1939– author.
Description: Series statement: Inanna F.A.R. art series | Includes bibliographical references.
Identifiers: Canadiana (print) 20200210653 | Canadiana (ebook) 20200210688 | ISBN 9781771337731 (softcover) | ISBN 9781771337748 (epub) | ISBN 9781771337755 (Kindle) | ISBN 9781771337762 (pdf)
Subjects: LCSH: National Ballet of Canada—History. | LCSH: Ballet companies—Canada—History. | LCSH: Ballet—Canada—History.
Classification: LCC GV1786.N38 A45 2020 | DDC 792.80971—dc23

This book is dedicated to Peter,
whose silence was always supportive.

Table of Contents

O chestnut-tree, great-rooted blossomer,
Are you the leaf, the blossom, of the bole?
O body swayed to music, O brightening glance,
How can we know the dancer from the dance?
　　　　—William Butler Yeats, "Among School Children"

Foreword

Those of us who have enjoyed long and satisfying careers through the most recent decades at the National Ballet of Canada owe an enormous debt of gratitude to the pioneers who came before us. It is wonderful to read of the trials, tribulations, and triumphs of those early years, and to imagine how different it must have been when the Company was first founded in the fifties.

The first-person accounts you are about to read conjure the sights, the smells, and the sweat that contributed to the National Ballet's formative years. The tributes written to those who have left us exemplify the kindness and courage that formed the foundations of the National Ballet.

A huge thank you to all who contributed to bring this important part of our history to life, and a special thank you to Jocelyn Terell Allen for the Herculean effort she undertook to compile these stories in *Early Days, Early Dancers*.

To those whose shoulders we all stand upon—many, many thanks.

—Karen Kain, C.C, LL.D., D.Litt., O.Ont.,
Artistic Director, National Ballet of Canada, September 2019

AT

**T
O
R
O
N
T
O**

1956

From
June 18

To
August 4

inclusive

School
Principal:
Betty
Oliphant

Announcing
the
SIXTH

*National
Ballet
Summer
School*

SCHOOL
DIRECTOR:

CELIA
FRANCA

Intensive 10 day courses for Teachers.

Full 7 weeks courses for Advanced, Intermediate and Basic students in R.A.D. and Cecchetti Syllabi. Pas-de-deux, Character, Variations, Labanotation, Music Appreciation.

Special courses for children of 8 years and over.

Evening classes for business girls.

Supervised accommodation will be available for young students.

For further information and prospectus write to:

Miss Yvette Thibaudeau
National Ballet Guild of Canada
73 Adelaide Street West, Toronto, Ont.

1.
Introduction

TWO STRONG WOMEN WERE INSTRUMENTAL in making the National Ballet of Canada what it is today. Under the leadership of Celia Franca, a woman of great drive and ambition, a humble ballet company was born in 1951, giving its first performance at the Eaton Auditorium on November 12th of that year. Throughout those early years, next to Celia Franca stood Betty Oliphant, a driving, exacting teacher who moulded many of the Company's early dancers, stoking their passion for ballet as children, and later as ballet mistress and head of the National Ballet School. Now, the National Ballet Company thrives under the artistic directorship of Karen Kain, herself a graduate of the National Ballet School in 1969.

In order to celebrate the people who together laid the foundation of the National Ballet of Canada, this book looks back to the 1950s. The focus of the book is on the dancers. As well, the book gives enormous credit to those who supported these early dancers: the directors, teachers, trainers, and choreographers. The body of the book comes from a questionnaire which was compiled and sent to twenty-four women and men who made up this original company, asking them to draw on their memories of those early years, using the following categories:

• What first inspired you to dance?
• What was your dance training prior to the National Ballet?
• Describe some of your performances and experiences of touring.

•What were your favourite and not-so-favourite ballets in the Company's repertoire?
•What were some of the most memorable and most terrifying moments of your life in the Company?
•Which dancers in the Company did you most admire?
•Describe your transition out of dance.

One of the Company's early dancers, Myrna Aaron, describes Toronto in the fifties as "rather dreary and provincial—not at all like the metropolis it is today." Nevertheless, along with other areas of growth in the performing arts in Canada, this "provincial" city was the birthplace of the National Ballet of Canada. This book tells the stories of the people, performances, talent, hard work, dedication, determination, and support that went into this development in the early years of the 1950s. These stories are told in the voices of the dancers who were a central part of these early years. They show firsthand how a group of dancers found a footing, overcoming almost insurmountable obstacles, to create what is now the world-class National Ballet of Canada. Throughout the book, the reader will come to understand the interlocking and interdependent roles of directors, teachers, choreographers, and most of all, the dancers. And the reader will come to appreciate all of the support and generosity provided for these dancers by families, schoolteachers, dance instructors, and each other.

By the summer of 1951, Celia Franca had gathered a group of dancers from across Canada. According to Franca, they were "half-trained" and trained in different styles, but "out of that summer school [in 1951] we got this little group of kids together to start the National Ballet Company—on nothing!" (Tennant, *Celia Franca*). The broader stories of the dancers unfold throughout this book: those who left school at age fourteen because they were determined to dance; those who appeared to already have the makings of prima ballerinas; those whose early years were marred by tragedies of the Second World War; and those whose families and teachers went to great lengths to show faith in their dreams.

How did this all begin? Boris Volkoff had a ballet studio in downtown Toronto at 777 Yonge Street, near the intersection at

Bloor Street, known as the Boris Volkoff Ballet. A plaque can still be found near that address today. His goal was to bring ballet to the masses and he presented dance and other performance acts from various cultural backgrounds to an eager Toronto audience. In 1934, he attracted a crowd of 5,500 to the Toronto Varsity Stadium to see one of his "bric-a-brac entertainments" (Morrison). At this time, Volkoff was asked by Mr. P.J. Mulqueen, head of the Sports Committee for Canada, to put together a group of dancers to compete at an international dance competition held in Germany, concurrent with the Berlin Olympics in 1936, where ultimately Volkoff's dancers performed with great success.

In 1950, three women from Toronto—Sydney Mulqueen, Pearl Whitehead, and Aileen Woods—consulted Boris Volkoff about establishing a national ballet company. Stewart James was manager of Volkoff's Canadian Ballet Studio and was one of those pursuing the possibilities for further development of ballet in Canada. From Russia originally, Volkoff had travelled through China, India, and other eastern countries as well as the United States as a ballet dancer and choreographer before settling in Canada. He believed that it would be advantageous for Canadian ballet, led by Volkoff's Canadian Ballet Studio, to take their dancers to some eastern countries to perform, and he and Stewart James were exploring these possibilities between 1948 and 1950. As well, James conducted a survey to determine the feasibility of ballet performances going on the Ontario touring circuit.

The next step was for Mulqueen, Whitehead, and Woods to raise funds to send Stewart James to Europe in search of an artistic director for what they envisioned as a future National Ballet of Canada. Specifically, he was directed to Dame Ninette deValois, who was at that time the artistic director of the Sadler's Wells Ballet in London (later the Royal Ballet), for her advice. deValois strongly recommended Celia Franca for the job. She called Franca "a strong dramatic dancer and very musical, and with teaching and choreographic experience" (Neufeld 36). James was suitably impressed with Franca and hired her to come to Canada to assess the possibilities of a Canadian national ballet company.

Meanwhile Mulqueen, Whitehead, and Woods worked with others to form a Women's Committee, known as the National

SHOULD YOU SUPPORT BALLET?

Is it really important that Canada have a national ballet company?

One capable of taking its place among the leading companies of North America?

A great many other Canadians think so. They have had sufficient faith in the National Ballet Company of Canada to help in its giant strides of the last five years.

Talented Canadians in a truly Canadian setting are accepted now as part of the major theatrical world. From a small company formed a few short years ago with plenty of courage and big ideas, but woefully inadequate funds, the National Ballet of Canada now is a full-size ballet organization, complete with its own orchestra, a rich repertoire of classics, contemporary works and original Canadian ballets.

Now we are appealing for your support. It is important that a sustaining fund of $150,000 be realized. The campaign opened Jan. 16.

This company will continue to expand. From the small hamlets of this country to the leading theatres of Montreal, Toronto, Vancouver, Halifax, New York, Washington and other cities it is known as the Canadian ballet company.

It is constantly providing a source of inspiration, by its very existence, to the youth of this country.

Canada is a vigorous, expanding country. Its young dancers, composers, artists and all the others interested in a career in this country need their opportunity.

They look to you for support.

An important ballet company, presenting the finest works available on a large scale, cannot live by the box-office alone. Pre-season rehearsals, new ballet costumes, stage settings, orchestrations and inter-provincial tours are expensive.

These are a few reasons you should support the National Ballet and why it is important that Canada have a company to absorb and inspire its talent and represent it artistically to the world.

Please send contribution to:

National Ballet of Canada

73 WELLINGTON ST. W.

TORONTO, ONTARIO

(Contributions are deductible for Income Tax purposes)

Ballet Guild. Their mandate was to raise money to bring Franca to Canada and to finance the first performance of the company in November 1951. It was also to encourage interest in the ballet, to garner broad support, and to raise funds through such activities as fashion shows, supper dances, ballet lectures, and demonstrations.

When Franca came to Canada in 1950 she toured coast-to-coast, locating dance studios and teachers, auditioning dancers, and attending a ballet festival in Montreal. She decided that a national ballet company was definitely possible. After first establishing a summer school in 1951, the new company premiered on November 12, 1951, at the Eaton Auditorium in Toronto. The program was Mikhail Fokine's *Les Sylphides*—a stylistic challenge for those young dancers who had grown up on traditional narrative ballets like *Sleeping Beauty* and *Polovtsian Dances* from Borodin's *Prince Igor*. Principal dancers were Celia Franca, Irene Apiné and Jury Gotshalks, and Lois Smith and David Adams.

How did this group of "half-trained kids" from across Canada manage to be on stage within a few months to dance at the Eaton Auditorium? The person at the centre of this development was, without a doubt, Celia Franca. She was unquestionably the Company's *force majeure* in those early days. There were others who were important: Betty Oliphant, ballet mistress, teacher of class, rehearser of ballets; Shirley Kash who taught class through thick and thin on tour; Grant Strate, the Company's first resident choreographer; and Kay Ambrose, another woman from England who did everything from preparing costumes and sets to calming dancers' nerves between acts.

You will read of a Celia who, as an artist, inspired the dancers with her own dancing. Celia, sublimely musical, trying to explain some intricacy of the music without counting; Celia who did not suffer fools gladly, getting impatient with her motley crew of dancers; Celia showing incredible stamina in the difficult job of founding a major ballet company. She had to deal with her board of directors, and beg desperately for funds in front of the theatre curtain at the end of a performance. She was unfazed, at least on the surface, with the greenness and inexperience of her dancers. She poured herself totally into coaching sessions with soloists. She was a woman of vision who could see much farther ahead than anyone else.

PAS DE DEUX CLASS

Vicki Bertram, circa 1950s. Courtesy: Private collection.

2.
Places and Spaces

THE PEOPLE OF TORONTO had been enjoying music, theatre, and concerts since the early years of the city's development. A search for concert halls available for performance in 1950 shows a sizeable list, including some that are still in use. The Danforth Music Hall was originally constructed as a movie theatre in 1919. It has a varied history, at one time being used as a Greek language theatre.

Of course, these places had funders and audiences, attuned to the local culture and bringing new culture with them. Massey Hall opened its doors at the corner of Yonge Street and Shuter Street in 1894 and held its first concert in June of that year. It was financed by Hart Massey of the well-known Massey-Harris Company, producers of farm equipment. Its goal as a music hall was to serve both rich and poor, with tickets selling for one dollar. The Masonic Temple at the corner of Yonge Street and Davenport Road opened on New Year's Day, 1918, and over the years was used by numerous groups and for numerous activities. In the 1930s it functioned as a ballroom and in the 1960s it began hosting a number of popular music groups.

The Great Hall at Queen Street and Dovercourt opened in 1899, constructed for the YMCA by chairman and local businessman, Samuel J. Moore. It was then sold to the Royal Templars of Temperance who later merged with the Independent Order of Foresters. In the 1940s it became the headquarters for the Polish National Union where Oldyna Dynowska, an original member of the National Ballet of Canada, began her dancing career. The Young Men's Hebrew Association eventually took over this space and, in 1951, offered it to Celia Franca as a place where the fledging ballet company could teach and practice. Prior to joining the company, Marcel Chojnacki had discovered that the YMHA offered modern interpretive dance classes and had joined them.

These businessmen, heads of corporations, and women's groups were community leaders. They facilitated culture and the arts in turn-of-the-century Toronto by providing funding and large spaces, such as the Masonic Temple and Massey Hall, to enable the arts to grow and develop in the city. They, and others, were still there in 1950 to help the National Ballet Company get its start. Celia Franca did not begin in a vacuum, but within a group of businesses and community organizations that valued and supported the arts in a multitude of ways.

Oldyna Dynowska, another early dancer, relates some interesting examples of how other businesses lent a hand. In the first year, the National Ballet was underwritten by Canadian companies such as Labatt's Brewery and Borden Dairy, with their famous Elsie the Cow image, who had been delivering dairy products to Canadians since 1867. In the early years of the National Ballet, Borden Dairy supplied vitamins and powdered milk to the dancers to keep them healthy. As well, Dynowska states that, "at Molson's Brewery, we dancers lined up with the truck drivers and other employees of Molson's to pick up our meagre dancer's pay." Other supporters behind the scenes showed their dedication to the Ballet Guild and the board of directors with time and money. Dynowska remembers "one name from the board, Mr. Goodman, who was a staunch supporter of Miss Franca and her efforts to form a company."

In contrast to Myrna Aaron's view of Toronto, another dancer, Katrina Evanova, whose family came from Bulgaria, found the city "a blaze of dazzling light" at night and full of adventure every day. Whether shopping at Eaton's (founded in 1869) or Simpson's (1858), attending a concert at Massey Hall (1894), or visiting the Royal Museum (1912) and Art Gallery of Ontario (1903), she and her family discovered a city full of activity, arts, and culture.

I describe these buildings and their founders to show that many powerful and wealthy men and women took an early interest not only in Toronto's economic development, but also in the cultural and artistic side of the growing city. In addition, these people represented a fairly large constituency of patrons of the arts, those who enjoyed theatre, music, and dance. Celia Franca was welcomed into this community who supported her by becoming members of her board, assisting in fundraising, and perhaps most of all, by becoming the audiences at the early performances of the National Ballet of Canada.

There are three locations that hold particular importance for the early months and years of the developing ballet company: Eaton Auditorium, the Royal Alexandra Theatre, and St. Lawrence Hall. In 1931, as well as having established the main department store at Queen and Yonge, Timothy Eaton opened another impressive store at College and Yonge, known as Eaton's College. The Art Deco-designed restaurant and concert hall on the seventh floor, known as the Auditorium and Round Room, is now a National Historic Site. The importance of this space for Celia Franca was that it included a concert hall. And in November 1951, this concert hall was the site of the National Ballet's first performance.

The Royal Alexandra Theatre was completed in 1907, on King Street west of University Avenue. It was designed by John McIntosh Lyle for a group of businessmen, led by Toronto's Cawthra Mulock, a twenty-one-year-old foundry owner, and millionaire from inherited wealth, who was determined to provide a modern centre for the performing arts. Other businessmen involved in the development of the Royal Alexandra Theatre included: Robert Alexander Smith, former president of The Toronto Stock Exchange; Stephen Haas, a manufacturer; and Lawrence Solman, owner of a baseball team, amusement park, and the Toronto Island ferries (Brockhouse). Starting in 1953, with the ballet *Lilac Garden*, by Antony Tudor, the Royal Alex became an early centre for the National Ballet performances. In the film, *The Dancers' Story*, dancer Lawrence Adams recalls: "One of the major moments for the National Ballet was in the late 1950s when we used to play at the Royal Alexandra Theatre and we had a six-week season there. It was absolutely extraordinary to play in the same theatre, to repeat these ballets over and

St. Lawrence Hall, 1951.
Courtesy: Lois Smith Electronic Archives at Dance Collection Danse.

Lilian Jarvis, Judie Colpman, Yves Cousineau, and Lois Smith in class at Pape Hall.
Courtesy: Lois Smith Electronic Archives at Dance Collection Danse.

over" (Tennant, *Dancers' Story*). The building that held the most precious memories for these early dancers was St. Lawrence Hall, on the southwest corner of King Street and Jarvis Street. After the great fire of 1849 had destroyed much of the lower east side of Toronto, St. Lawrence Hall was opened in 1850. On the third floor was an event space that was one hundred feet long, thirty-eight feet wide and thirty-six feet high, with a magnificent gas chandelier. It was considered the only place in Toronto at that time for lectures, such as those by abolitionist Frederick Douglass, and fashionable concerts, such as that of Jenny Lind, the "Swedish Nightingale," in October of 1851.

However, by the turn of the century, the centre of the city had shifted westwards and the St. Lawrence Hall had gone by the wayside. By 1950, it was covered in grime and dirt, windows were broken, and the exterior structure was starting to crumble. Several rooms were occupied by homeless people. According to an article written by Chris Bateman in 2016 and published in *Spacing Toronto*, "When the National Ballet moved into the upper floors in the 1950s, it started a long conversation about how to properly restore the building." The St. Lawrence Hall was beautifully restored, and the birth of the Ballet played a major role in the decision to begin its restoration.

A number of places were on offer to help the burgeoning National Ballet for their classes and rehearsals, for example, church basements and other ballet studios such as one run by Boris Volkoff.

Nevertheless the training and rehearsing of these early dancers was primarily, though not exclusively, at St. Lawrence Hall, the gateway to the National Ballet. In spite of its poor condition, these beginning dancers took the building on as their own, showing great humour and great affection for the space. Edelayne Brandt is one of many dancers who talk about "that magic green door" and "the long, winding stairway to the second floor ... with windows overlooking a massive hall of fruit and vegetable stands. Then came the stairway to heaven, to the once-elegant old concert hall where the National Ballet had daily classes and rehearsals." Victoria Bertram recalls early days of classes: "I was faced with a wide, grey, well-worn, dimly-lit wood staircase leading up to a second floor. It creaked as I ascended timidly, heart pounding." Myrna Aaron remembers St. Lawrence Hall as, "Marvellous! Now it has been restored to its original historic self, but back then, it was filthy, housed rats, various smells, and sometimes birds that flew into the huge windows upstairs where Jenny Lind once sang." Judie Colpman describes it as "huge ... the biggest studio I had ever seen. I loved it immediately and always did.... There was enough space to accommodate two full casts at the same time with ample space on the fringe for individual work." Celia Franca, Betty Oliphant, and other VIPs sat at the front of the room, their backs to the stage and a wider mirror, watching and directing rehearsals. The dancers rehearsed facing Celia and Betty after they had warmed-up class using barres on pedestals in the centre of the room, which would later be moved off to the sides. Bob Ito remembers one great occasion when the Bolshoi Ballet Company came to Toronto and used the St. Lawrence Hall for classes and rehearsals. The Toronto dancers were thrilled to watch legendary dancers such as Galina Ulanova, Maya Plisetskaya, and many of the soloists and dancers take class.

As much as the dancers talk about the broken windows where birds flew in and out, the ubiquitous dirt, and the occasional rats, they agreed that the old wood floor was wonderful to dance on and that they loved the place. Angela Leigh states: "The space, the room itself, the feeling there with the windows and the feeling of history, that was absolutely wonderful. The memory has not left me" (Tennant, *Dancers' Story*). Victoria Bertram recalls the "couple of sets of grey, steel bunk beds with very questionable mattresses, which occasionally the Scott Mission would use for men with no homes of their own. I shudder to think back then that we used these to sit on, eat our lunches, chat or take short naps!" Victoria continues with a description of the washrooms, with a rusty metal trough as the washing basin, and high-mounted taps that dripped all the time. The toilets were raised up on blocks with rectangles of burlap that were hung around each one to create makeshift stalls. "Very rustic" she calls it.

The National Ballet used the St. Lawrence Hall for most of the year. However, in the winter months, the Hall was still used to house indigent men and the Company had to relocate to a second-floor studio on Pape Avenue. According to Donald Mahler, that space could not be heated because the first floor stored hay and fodder, and the landlord was worried about fires. The dancers felt very lucky to have the wonderful St. Lawrence Hall with its magnificent wood floor to rehearse in the rest of the year. Every subsequent space was unfavourably compared to it.

Donald Mahler adds, "In later years the building was renovated and brought back to its former glory. One day in those after-years I went with Miss Franca to revisit the scene of our former toils. We looked around and at each other and we both had the same thought. She said to me, 'Yes, I liked it better then, too.'"

Vicki Bertram, circa 1950s. Courtesy: Private collection.

Vicki Bertram, circa 1950s. Courtesy: Private collection.

Celia Franca and David Adams in Dark of the Moon.
Courtesy of the National Ballet Archives.

3.
Early Training

IMAGINE THAT YOU WANTED TO DANCE more than anything else in the world, and that Celia Franca, a dancer from the revered Sadler's Wells Ballet of London has come from England to form a Canadian ballet company. This company could be your one chance to dance professionally in Canada. As artistic director, Franca has the final say about who will dance with her company. How was this small group of dancers able to take advantage of that chance, perhaps the only chance? There are two basic questions to consider here: Where did the motivation come from? Who and what enabled them to take advantage of this life-changing opportunity?

First, it is important to place these stories into an historical context. The year 1950, when Franca agreed to come to Canada and face this monumental task, was ten years after the end of the Depression of the 1930s, and only five years after the end of World War II. Partly because of these tragic conditions, Canada had opened its doors to hundreds of thousands of immigrants. They were fleeing war-torn Europe and bringing their energy and culture with them to late 1940s and early 1950s Canada. According to the Canada Year Book, over one million immigrants entered Canada between January 1946 and June 1954. The total population had gone from just over twelve million to just over fifteen million. This arrival of talent and culture and energy provided an opportunity for Canada to grow not only in population, but also in industry, economics, and the arts. Many of these early dancers and their teachers had a connection to the people, events, and cultures of Europe.

For some of the dancers, World War II had a personal and horrific impact. Marcel Chojnacki was born in Brussels in 1932. When Hitler invaded Belgium in 1940, most of Marcel's family, which included six children, were sent to the concentration camps and their deaths. He and two of his brothers spent the remaining war years in orphanages. When they came to Canada in 1947, they settled in Toronto with other Jewish orphans. In the spring of 1948, Marcel went to see a movie called *The Red Shoes*. This film is based on a fairy tale by Hans Christian Andersen, in which a young ballerina joins a ballet company and becomes the lead dancer in a ballet called *The Red Shoes*. Marcel was enthralled by the role of the Shoemaker, performed by the Russian dancer, Leonide Massine, who choreographed his own part in the film. Marcel decided on the spot that he wanted to be able to create the kind of magic that Massine had created in the film. He stated, "I danced and leapt out of the movie theatre that day thinking, 'That's the life for me!'"

His first step was to find a studio and a teacher. Marcel started his training at the Young Men's Hebrew Association in modern interpretive dance classes, which used the Martha Graham technique. He also joined the New Dance Theatre. Most importantly, Marcel discovered Boris Volkoff's ballet company. "Boris Volkoff made it possible for me to come as often as I was able" for reduced fees. He then studied with Betty Oliphant, who was teaching along with Celia Franca. With this solid background, he was accepted into the Sadler's Wells Ballet in London for training during the years 1954 and 1955. One of his teachers there was Harold Turner, a ballet master who had a Saturday morning class for men. Upon his return to Toronto, he joined the National Ballet.

The Laine Metz School of Ballet in Edmonton was based on the teaching methods established by Mary Wigman in Germany in the early part of the twentieth century. Laine Metz had performed with Mary Wigman, in Europe. Metz fled Estonia after the War and when she arrived in Edmonton, she opened the Laine Metz School of Ballet, bringing the rigorous Eastern European teaching methods to her Canadian students. One of her top students was Grant Strate, later a founding member of the National Ballet of Canada, and the Company's first resident choreographer.

Another Laine Metz student was Edelayne Brandt. Brandt hadn't planned to become a dancer. "I simply danced my way into it," she says. It was fortunate that her family moved to Edmonton; at ten years old she was enrolled in the Laine Metz School. Celia Franca was so impressed with her skills when she first saw Brandt perform in a small recital that she asked her parents if the young student could come to Toronto to study with Betty Oliphant. Brandt's parents thought twelve was a bit too young to leave her family and move halfway across the country for ballet lessons. A year later, when she was thirteen, Franca made the request again, and this time Brandt's parents agreed. Soon, she was on a train to Toronto accompanied by Laine Metz. Then, because she was so young, her parents decided, "generously and courageously," that the entire family would move to Toronto with her. One of the first people Brandt met at the summer school was an equally young, naïve, and terrified dancer, Jocelyn Botterell, whose stage name later became Jocelyn Terell.

Bob Ito started his career in the arts at age five when he won twenty-five dollars in a competition at the Pacific National Exhibition. When he was six years old he began studying singing, elocution, and tap dancing, and he began performing on radio programs and at festivals. However, like Marcel Chojnacki, Bob Ito's life was taken over by World War II. As a young Canadian boy, but one of Japanese origin, he and his entire family and community spent 1942 to 1946 in an internment camp at Tashme-Hope in British Columbia. After they were released, they were located to a farm in Alberta where he sang in the Mormon Children's Choir. Under martial law, the only city that they were allowed to live in was Montreal. This is where Bob began the study of ballet. His group, *Ballet Entre Nous*, was invited to attend the new National Ballet Summer School. From that summer school, five dancers from Montreal were selected by Celia Franca to join the newly established National Ballet: Marilyn Rollo, Brian Macdonald, Andrew Dufresne, Howard Meadows, and Bob Ito. As a young boy confined in an internment camp in British Columbia, Ito never dreamt that years later he would become a

Cecily Paige backstage in Le Carnavale!, *1957. Courtesy of National Ballet Archives.*

founding member of the National Ballet of Canada in Toronto.

Cecily Paige is another dancer whose training in London was interrupted by World War II. However, she did find an excellent teacher, Kathleen Yatos, a first-class Cecchetti ballet method teacher. Later Cecily had the good fortune to study at the Rambert

School at Notting Hill Gate. "[Marie] Rambert was a taskmaster, someone to be feared and worshipped in the same breath." Paige also had opportunities with the live television show, *Ballet for Beginners*, and was a fill-in when regular ballet dancers became ill or injured. She continued her training with the Royal Ballet School and the Royal Opera Ballet with Harold Turner in charge. She then had an offer from Celia Franca to join the National Ballet of Canada.

Pauline McCullagh began with very progressive early schools that offered music, rhythm, and movement. She claims that she "was hooked" on dancing from a young age. She was with the Ruth Sorel group and danced at the first Canadian Ballet Festival in a flooded Winnipeg "where I gawked at the talent and flexibility of a young Lynn Seymour" (a highly acclaimed Canadian ballerina). Her excellent training with Elizabeth Leese opened the door for McCullagh to be accepted by England's Royal Ballet School and be given a role in *Lady from the Sea,* a ballet later given to the National Ballet.

Donald Mahler had won a four-year scholarship to the Fine Arts Department of Syracuse University when he was given a book about the famous dancer, Vaslav Nijinsky. After reading this book, he became intrigued with ballet and attended a performance of the American Ballet Theatre, "which just about blew me away!" He followed a recommendation to study at the Metropolitan Opera Ballet School. Even though he had a muscle injury, he stayed with his dream of ballet. He gave up his fine-art scholarship and signed up for ballet classes in earnest at the Metropolitan Opera House. The school was directed by Antony Tudor, the great choreographer, and Margaret Craske, one of Enrico Cecchettis's favourite pupils. Celia Franca had worked with both of them in England in the 1930s, and had performed in Tudor's works at the Ballet Rambert. When the National Ballet of Canada came to New York in the spring of 1955, they asked for "supers" (onstage non-dancing performers) from the Met School. And as Mahler says "I made my 'debut' with the Company right then and there."

Shirley Kash was born in Toronto to a Hungarian father and a Russian mother. Music was part of their culture and she grew up

Shirley Kash. Courtesy: Private collection.

folk dancing. Both of her parents placed high value on music and dancing. Her father decided that she and her brothers should go to the Russian Hall, instead of the Hungarian Hall, for dancing and it was there that she met Boris Volkoff, "a Russian fellow, [who] was teaching ballet, and so I did a little bit of that with him." Kash was only eight or nine at the time and she found him "very strict." She adds: "You know, Russian teachers, they just push you and you would do everything, whether you really could or not." Her mother also took her to the Ukrainian Hall, where the character teacher (who taught stylized folk dance used in ballet and for theatrical performances) started with a half-hour of ballet. As well, their parents took Shirley and her brothers to the University Settlement House, near Grange Park and the Art Gallery of Ontario, where it cost only fifty cents for a half-hour of piano lessons. Cynthia Barrett, a modern dance teacher based in Toronto, had started a student scholarship in piano, violin, voice, and dance. Kash won the four-year scholarship for dance, and after that Cynthia Barrett recommended her to Betty Oliphant.

Lilian Jarvis points out that she came very close to missing the opportunity to dance with the National Ballet. Her Toronto ballet teacher, Millie Wickson, encouraged her to study with Boris Volkoff, "a local high-energy Russian teacher who had formed the Volkoff Canadian Ballet." Lilian went on tours with his company in Ontario, performed in New York City, and in the 1948 and 1949 Canadian Ballet Festivals. After this, Wickson took her and two other dancers to England for the summer months to study with Wickson's former teacher, Cleo Nordi. Jarvis stayed on when she got a chance to replace another dancer in the musical, *Carousel,* which was playing at the Theatre Royal on Drury Lane. For the next year, Lilian did eight shows a week, danced in Sunday productions at the Mercury Theatre, and took classes with the English "modern" ballet teacher, Audrey de Vos. Perhaps not surprisingly, she damaged her Achilles tendons and came back to Canada to recuperate, only to discover that Celia Franca had come to Toronto from London to start a new ballet company. At Millie Wickson's urging again, she auditioned for Celia Franca.

Janet Green Foster began ballet classes with the Ottawa Classical Ballet at age nine, where her teacher was Nesta Toumine. When her family moved to Washington, DC, she'd had the opportunity to see performances by the New York City Ballet, the American Ballet Theatre with Alicia Alonso, the Ballet Russe de Monte Carlo, and Sadler's Wells. She watched, entranced, as Margot Fonteyn and Michael Soames performed *Swan Lake.* "Between Acts II and III, I suddenly and unexpectedly announced to my father 'I want to go to England.'" With her parents' approval, at age fifteen, Janet sailed alone to England to study at the Elmhurst

Irene Apiné in Coppelia, *1954. Photo: Ken Bell. Courtesy National Ballet Archives.*

Ballet School in Camberly, Surrey. The classes were held in old Quonset Huts, pre-fabricated steel structures left over from the War. When Janet's father discovered that Celia Franca had established the National Ballet in Toronto, Janet returned to Toronto to study with Betty Oliphant.

Leila Zorina came with her family to Pier 21 in Halifax in 1951, from the refugee camps in Europe. She notes that other early dancers with the National Ballet also arrived in Canada through Pier 21 in Halifax, including Jury Gotshalks and Irene Apiné. Zorina's father, who had a doctorate in veterinary surgery from the University of Vienna, had arrived six months earlier and been working as a lumberjack. By the time the rest of the family arrived, he had settled in Montreal. Leila began ballet lessons at her elementary school, and after two years of Saturday classes,

Leila Zorina. Courtesy of the National Ballet Archives.

her teacher, Miss Fisher, suggested that she study at the Elizabeth Leese studio. Because her family could not afford the fees, for four years Leila attended Elizabeth Leese's studio on a scholarship.

Valerie Lyon grew up in Niagara Falls, Ontario, but her mother took her across the border to a Russian ballet teacher in Niagara Falls, New York. She was put *en pointe* too early, and withdrew from ballet for a few years as a result. Later she trained with Jean Spiers, a Cecchetti specialist, who recognized Valerie's talent and suggested that she go to the National Ballet Summer School to study with Betty Oliphant.

Valerie Lyon as Princess in Swan Lake, *1959.*
Courtesy: National Ballet Archives.

Oldyna Dynowska's story emphasizes the importance of the cultural underpinnings by which young people can find a path to becoming a professional ballet dancer, and the possibility of finding support for artistic dreams in unexpected places. As a young person in a Polish community, she attended social dances on Saturday nights. The dances were not the contemporary popular dances of the day, but Polish dances with Polish rhythms such as the Mazurka, Oberek, and so on. A teacher from Poland also taught them Polish dances for the stage, which as amateurs, they performed for the Polish community.

This led Dynowska to ballet. When she was in high school, preparing for entry into university, she also studied ballet on a working scholarship with Toronto teacher Bettina Byers, taking classes after school each evening and on weekends. Eventually she was called into the vice principal's office. "Mr. Skiro was a gruff and seemingly uncongenial man, and he questioned me about my falling grades and my goal in life. Learning of my desire to become a dancer, and how serious I was, he rearranged all my academic classes to be taken in the afternoon, freeing up the mornings so that I could study with Miss Byers, and I continued taking all the ballet classes after school as well." This was an unusual and farsighted accommodation by the school and a man in authority who might have been less than sympathetic, effectively demonstrating how the school system could accommodate young people with non-academic goals.

This brief look at the backgrounds of some of the early dancers places them in a very particular time historically: the end of World War II; the immigration of hundreds of thousands of newcomers to Canada and the importance of their cultural roots; the already established ballet teachers and studios as well as supportive community centres in various parts of Canada; the many parents who believed in and supported however possible the dreams of their children and teenagers; the dance teachers who found scholarships (or created them), provided free classes, and used their connections when they saw a dancer of promise. Another theme that runs throughout these dancers' stories is the desire to dance from a very young age, and the commitment they put into it, attending school all day long and then ballet classes five nights a week plus Saturdays. They not only dreamed to dance, but they lived to dance.

Gloria Bonnell, 1956-57 souvenir booklet.
Courtesy: Private collection.

4.
Learning on the Job

M OST OF THE DANCERS I CONTACTED spoke at length about the amount of learning and practice that went into becoming a ballet dancer. As noted in the previous chapter, they came to the National Ballet Company with various skills, training, and experiences in the world of ballet. The first connection to the National Ballet was often through classes with Betty Oliphant. Several dancers acknowledge that without Betty Oliphant's generosity and strict teaching, they would never have moved from the summer school to the Company. It was through her that they reached Celia Franca.

Not only was she a rigorous teacher, but Betty Oliphant was personally kind to, and supportive of, upcoming ballerinas. Gloria Bonnell, along with her sister Carol, met Miss O. (as she was affectionately called), through her daughters. They had early training with Helen and Fanny Birdsall where they were taught ballet, toe, acrobatics, and tap. Since her parents did not have "a potty to piddle in," as Bonnell puts it, she and her sister were invited to attend classes at the summer school, for two weeks, free of charge. In the fall, they both began to study ballet with Oliphant at her Sherbourne Street studio, still free of charge, but with some small duties in exchange. Bonnell explains, "Every day I went straight to the studio from school, made tea for Miss O., fed Butterscotch (Miss O.'s cat), did this and that. In return I attended as many classes as were available." Cathy Carr was another young student trained and supported by Betty Oliphant. From Thornhill, north of Toronto, Cathy was only fourteen in tenth grade, and fainted during her first class at the National Ballet

Celia Franca and Kay Ambrose, 1951-1952 tour.
Courtesy: Lois Smith Electronic Archive at Dance Collection Danse.

Summer School. Betty Oliphant took her under her wing, and let her live in her house with her two children. Carr remembers, "She was a wonderful person and a mentor, although strict and intimidating. She had my undying respect. Joining the Company was a rather daunting and frightening experience for me and my parents, but we accepted the honour and endured the hardships." Before Marcel Chojnacki travelled to London to spend a year at Sadler's Wells, he had been studying with Betty Oliphant. When he returned to Canada to join the National Ballet Company, Betty Oliphant and Celia Franca were his principal ballet masters for classes and rehearsals.

When Janet Green Foster's father discovered that Celia Franca had established the National Ballet in Toronto, he arranged for her to return to Toronto to study with Betty Oliphant. Through Betty Oliphant, Janet Green Foster and many other incoming dance students were recommended to Celia Franca and subsequently invited to join the Company.

Kay Ambrose was another major influence in the early days of the Company. She was invited to join the Company from England where she had worked with Celia Franca. She was already known to many of the dancers because of her book, *The Ballet Lover's Pocket-book*. Ambrose taught the young students how to apply stage make-up and classical hairstyles for particular ballets. Myrna Aaron describes her as a woman always with a cigarette in her mouth, her clothes full of holes from the ashes she dropped on them. She is remembered as having a genuine love for the dancers, always feeding them. Myrna relates that, "Many years later I ran into her in London and she immediately took me to a restaurant." Nevertheless, Celia Franca was the dominant person in their classes and rehearsals. Celia Franca was a teacher, an artistic director, and a woman of vision, capable of imagining this disjointed group of would-be dancers coming together in performance. One of the ways she taught was to dance with the students in classes and rehearsals, and to perform with them onstage when necessary. Myrna Aaron provides some enlightening detail. "What a job Celia had taken on! She taught class every morning, dancing most of it along with us as she was still performing at the time. It must have been a daunting task to try to whip us into a cohesive style. In addition, she also taught us the ballets we would perform for our debut performances and subsequent mini-tours." Aaron elaborates on Franca's expertise, which she passed on to her students. "Known for her musicality, she taught us not only technique, but how to shade and accent movement the way a musician plays music, a concept which was entirely new to me. Just as not all the notes in a musical score are given the same stress or importance, so it is with dance steps. Celia put us on the path from mere execution to what one might describe as artistry." As well as being taught the mechanics of the dance steps, the nuances of their roles, and the importance of musicality, the dancers also learned by observing their teachers and the more experienced dancers perform. The more experienced dancers also often acted as mentors to the younger dancers. Edelayne Brandt provides a detailed account of Celia Franca as a teacher and a role model.

"I was in awe of Celia Franca, both as a gifted dancer and as our leader. She wore colourful and amusing teaching and rehearsal clothes, smoked constantly, made us laugh uproariously, or slink away in shame if we missed a step. Above all, she inspired us to try harder and do better. She wrangled and moulded her disparate collection of dancers—all shapes, sizes, and techniques."

Lilian Jarvis also recognized that as well as training the dancers to try harder and do better, Celia Franca had a vision of the National Ballet as one fluid body. When she went across the country looking for potential dancers, "technical prowess and physical suitability were not her criteria for acceptance. Rather, she looked mainly for qualities and personalities that she could mould and develop into something resembling uniformity." Janet Green Foster found Celia Franca different from her previous teachers, and she recognized that the difference came from the fact that Franca was doing more than most ballet teachers. Franca was creating a ballet company. "She was tough and demanding, but to create a ballet company, she had to be. She was also a stickler for perfection. Her tongue could be sharp, particularly with comments and criticism to dancers in her class. In her presence, one was easily intimidated, but always challenged to do better."

Bob Ito remembers his first week of rehearsing when the men, who were not used to the intense movements that Franca demanded they learned, found that every muscle in their body was "one big ache." He describes how they "could barely get on the streetcar—the conductor had to wait for us to crawl on." A number of the dancers realized that they were doing more than just joining a ballet company, they were helping to create a ballet company. Therefore, Betty Oliphant and Celia Franca were strict with them, demanding perfectionists. As well, the early dancers were devoted to one another, and recognized they had to do exceptionally well because of their responsibility to each other.

The student dancers were aware of Oliphant and Franca acting not just as teachers, but as mentors. They also recognized they could learn from the more experienced dancers and even each other. Cathy Carr calls Betty Oliphant a "wonderful person and mentor." She also admired the skills of Lilian Jarvis. "Lilian Jarvis dancing in *L'apres midi d'un faune* was one of my favourite performances. More than the fact that she was a prima ballerina, it was the feminine beauty of her dancing that spoke to my heart."

Marcel Chojnacki gives credit to the other dancers from whom he learned a great deal by his careful observation of how they danced. He includes in this list: Lois Smith, Lilian Jarvis, Angela Leigh, David Adams, Celia Franca, and Betty Pope, who danced with Adams and Smith in *The Nutcracker* on CBC television. Gloria Bonnell states that she "was in awe of several of the National's dancers back then, both male and female. However, from the very first time I saw Lilian Jarvis, I just loved to watch her dance. She was my idol, and she still is to this day."

Judie Colpman had been studying dance with Bettina Byers at the Royal Academy of Dance in Toronto. Her stepfather gave her the tuition money to attend the National Ballet's summer school as a graduation gift. Judie describes her first meeting with Celia Franca: "Before me was a beautiful, exotic woman with thick black hair in a single braid wound around her head like a Russian headdress. Her dark brown eyes made up with black kohl were warm and scrutinizing. She wore a dark blue shirt and long pants, black socks and sandals peeked out from under her trousers, and she smoked a long cigarette. We liked each other immediately and we hugged. For some reason, I was never afraid of her, unlike many of my fellow dancers. Angry, yes, but she was my boss. The Boss."

Judie goes on to discuss the importance of the musicians whom Franca "used brilliantly" to help teach them the rules of counting, being "on the music" and learning to let the music inform their steps and emotions, of "the feeling " of moving with the music. As Judie explains it, "Summer School was an ecstatic time."

Yves Cousineau had a great desire to perform and had some experience with walk-on parts in plays in Montreal. One of his teachers, who introduced him to the basic rules of movement and mime, suggested that he consider ballet. He was invited by Elizabeth Leese, who had the finest studio in Montreal, to take some classes. When he informed her that he had no money, she suggested that he could come for free if he never missed a class. And he never did.

Elizabeth Leese and Brian Macdonald choreographed a number of dance and variety shows for television, where Yves met some of the dancers from the National Ballet in Toronto. He was most impressed with Lois Smith and David Adams. These dancers mentored him during the summer school at St. Lawrence Hall. Not having much money, he attended all the classes he could for two weeks. This is when he was introduced to Celia Franca and Betty Oliphant. As Yves explains it, "I came back home exceedingly excited by all these people, the huge studio, and the ease of taking classes with such advanced dancers. Elizabeth received a letter from Celia asking her if I would be interested in becoming an apprentice with a contract of thirty to thirty-five dollars per week. The urge to be there again was very strong. I accepted the offer. I was not in any way a professional dancer, but I would keep on training—learning a repertoire and being onstage."

Although Yves did not speak English fluently, he was supported by the other dancers, and made friends. He and fellow dancer, Bob Ito, shared a room on Homewood Street. "Bob was a great performer and a true friend." The student dancers began to understand the intense degree to which ballet is not a solitary pursuit; a company had to perform as a moving entity, the dancers interconnected with one another. Part of the learning was how to make that connection. And the support they learned to show one another would create cohesion.

Valerie Lyon remembers the quality of the Company in those days, the freshness and joy among the dancers. She recalls that there was no snobbery. "We worked together and were obedient to Celia. We were all willing to sacrifice ourselves in order to contribute. The dancers worked hard in this tough life. It wasn't play—we worked hard. But it was a great experience. We woke early, travelled many miles by bus. We went the extra mile."

Oldyna Dynowska describes the necessity for this company-wide bond in the early days. "In the first years of the National Ballet, there was no star system. We were all on the same level and as a result, we were a very cohesive group. In about the third year the schisms started to appear as distinctions and ambitions emerged. But a company is based on the efforts of all of its members, not just its stars, and we were still a very dedicated and striving group of dancers ... the sacrifices, the dedication, and the perseverance of those first dancers, and the hardworking champions of those first years, all laid a foundation for the possibility of a Canadian Ballet."

Edelayne Brandt expands on the importance of support within the Company. "We were a close-knit, caring, supportive troupe. We'd cheer from the wings when one of us debuted a solo and cross our fingers for success when presenting a new ballet. We were all thrilled to be in the Company and were willing to work very, very hard. Our tour reviews were usually favourable, often referring to us as a young, fresh-faced, and well-rehearsed company".

Over the months and years of classes and rehearsals, and of course performances they learned not only to dance, but to bond as one unit, one Company.

Brian Macdonald and Teresa Mann gesture to Celia Franca on the train, 1952.
Courtesy: Myrna Aaron Electronic Archives at Dance Collection Danse.

5.

Performances and Touring

ALL OF THIS WORK, OF COURSE, was to lead to the stage, and some of the dancers were onstage that first summer. Myrna Aaron describes a Promenade concert at Varsity Arena with the Toronto Symphony Orchestra. Lois Smith and David Adams did the peasant *pas de deux* from *Giselle*, then Celia Franca danced as Swanhilda in *Coppelia*. "That fall, those of us who danced *Giselle,* along with a few other dancers, formed the first company of the Canadian National Ballet, later the National Ballet of Canada." At the same time as they were still being trained as professional dancers, they were debuting onstage for live audiences, and, according to Myrna, being greeted "very warmly." The Company officially began in September 1951, and their first performance was in the Eaton Auditorium in November 1951. The dancers had daily classes and rehearsals to learn the repertoire for *Les Sylphides, Salome,* the *Giselle pas de deux, Étude,* and the Polovtsian dances from *Prince Igor.* They were ready for the opening and had a very positive reception.

In January 1953, Antony Tudor had come from England to choreograph at the Royal Alexandra Theatre on King Street West in Toronto. Judie Colpman says that working with him was "life-altering" for her. She was particularly impressed with the exquisite and dramatic dancing in *Lilac Garden.* "Tudor worked us hard on what it was like to step, to dance on grass, how the scent of lilacs affected us. This is what I wanted: to create the movement from both the narrative and the music in a more natural way. But his choreography was technically specific." One of Bob Ito's favourite memories was in the summer of 1953 when

David Adams and Natalia Butko in Étude, *1951.*
Courtesy: National Ballet Archives.

the Company was invited to perform in Jacob's Pillow Dance Festival in the Berkshires in Massachusetts. They performed Tudor's *Lilac Garden, L'apres midi d'un faune,* and the second act of *Casse-Noisette.* Jury Gotshalks and Irene Apiné performed *Don Quixote's pas de deux,* and Lois Smith and David Adams performed *Giselle's* peasant *pas de deux.*

Edelayne Brandt describes her first performance. "The opening night of my career took place in St. Catharines, Ontario. Miss Franca helped me with stage make-up and the other dancers onstage whispered instruction to me—turn left now, follow Oldyna, exit with Judie. In the sultry *danse arabe* of *The Nutcracker's* fourth act, I entered doing the splits on the shoulders of Howard Meadows and Glenn Gibson. There I was with bare midriff, sheer pantaloons, Miss Franca's exotic Indian jewellery, and only a vague notion of what 'sensuous' meant. Oh, how I loved it all!"

The dancers were not without humour at some of the near-disasters that befell them. Sally Brayley tells a funny story about performing at the Royal Alex in Toronto. "I was leading the line into our straight line upstage and pliéd into a fourth position, arms up in an arabesque position. As I took my position, I realized I was facing the wrong way so I carefully turned around and came nose-to-nose with Myrna, who immediately thought she was wrong and she turned and the whole line continued on a follow-up. When I realized my mistake, I turned back to my first side as did all the dancers in another follow. It was a disaster! Here I was, supposed to be the backbone of the *corps de ballet.* Even though I was mortified, I burst into laughter, as did the rest of the line."

Some of the performances left a lifelong impression on the dancers. Janet Green Foster states that those impressions are as clear now as they were then: "Franca's portrayal of *Giselle* in the mad scene sent shivers up my spine. So, too, did her performance in *Winter Night,* one of my favourite ballets, with its perfect blending of story, choreography, and Rachmaninoff's haunting second piano concerto. I remember Lois and David using the full sweep of the stage in an electrifying performance of *The Nutcracker* Act IV *pas de deux.* They were our premier dancers."

Bob Ito and Frank Rodwell.
Courtesy: Lois Smith Electronic Archives and Dance Collection Danse..

As Judie Colpman so aptly describes those early years, "the job was on the road. In his submission for this book, Bob Ito remembers the first couple of years and lists the many stops they made on their tours. They performed in Sudbury, Hamilton, Kitchener-Waterloo, London, Ottawa, Guelph, and Halifax. In subsequent years, they travelled across Canada by train to Sudbury, Winnipeg, Regina, Saskatoon, Lethbridge, Calgary, Edmonton, and Vancouver. In 1957/58 they performed in eight cities in Ontario and Quebec, then from Vancouver and Trail in British Columbia to Edmonton and Red Deer in Alberta, to Saskatoon in Saskatchewan. They also crossed the border to

Walla Walla in Washington, then San Francisco, Los Angeles, and eleven other cities in California plus eight cities in Texas. The last city to end this tour was Sudbury, Ontario.

After a nine-day break, they had what Judie calls the wonderful experience of Mexico City, "a miraculous three weeks" at the Palacio Bellas Artes and Auditorio Nacional in Chapultepec Park. "The Mexican audiences were ecstatic in their appreciation." On this marathon tour, they performed seventy-five times in one hundred and one days.

The 1957 tour stands out for Edelayne Brandt, opening on February 6 in Sioux Falls, South Dakota, and ending April 1 in Newark, New Jersey, having zigzagged through fifteen states in between. These were mostly one-night performances and the day would begin by boarding the bus by eight a.m., driving hundreds of miles, class at five p.m., and curtain time at eight p.m. Hopefully there would be a reception after the performance where the dancers would "gracefully swarm the food tables to augment our paycheques." Edelayne admits that, "bus travel and one-night stands can be brutal, but we had youth on our side. It was exhilarating and exciting!" The three young dancers— Edelayne, Jocelyn Terell, and Shirley Kash—had opportunities to see the Empire State Building and a show at Radio City Music Hall in New York; have a riverboat cruise down the Mississippi; and eat pecan pie in Louisiana, "with a wary eye out for Miss Franca—too fattening, too delicious. What a close, happy trio we were!"

Victoria Bertram describes her experience of a typical performance tour. Her example started in Concord, New Hampshire, and finished in Evansville, Indiana, after they had performed in twenty-one cities. "We made very little and while on tour were given an extra five dollars *per diem* to pay not only for our food, but our lodgings (a double room was about two dollars and fifty cents). But what heady days they were!"

Judie Colpman felt the tour bus was a refuge. On some of the buses the luggage rack was wide enough to sleep on. "To sleep, to think, to dream, especially out the window as night was swooping down and lights turned on in the windows of homes. In the early evening, life took place on the first floor, people moving from

Sally Brayley in Lilac Garden, *1961. Photo: Ken Bell.*
Courtesy: National Ballet Archives.

room to room, setting the table, serving dinner, lifting children up. But I always knew we would arrive at the theatre soon, find our dressing rooms, and begin the pre-performance ritual: class, rehearsal, makeup, costumes, onstage!"

One memory of touring by train is provided by Marilyn Rollo. She became very ill and was left in the railway car while the rest of the Company went to the theatre for their performance. During the night, while she was sleeping, the railway car was moved and the rest of them had a difficult time finding her. Marilyn says that, "I thought it was so funny, being in the railroad sidelots and completely lost. It was chaos for a bit, but all turned out all right in the end."

Although Judie experienced the bus as a place of safety and security, that was not always the case. One tour, while driving through the night, Yves Cousineau was standing in the well beside the driver to stretch his legs and talk to the driver to keep him alert, which they took turns doing during overnight drives. Just after Yves moved, the bus lurched and went off the road down a steep embankment with a creek at the bottom. The driver deliberately drove into a pole to prevent the bus from rolling over, and the pole came up in the well where Yves had been standing. It was a terrifying experience for the dancers, started awake, trying to gather their belongings, and climb out of windows. A new bus arrived and, though shaken up, they performed that evening.

Another time the bus malfunctioned and they had to wait for a replacement, which resulted in their being two hours late for performance time. The stagehands had their costumes and make-up ready and the kettle boiling for tea. The audience, already seated in the theatre, cheered and clapped on their arrival. It was agony for them to dance with cold ankles, no warm-up time. They received a standing ovation at the end of the performance and a rave review the next day.

Sally Brayley has a different memory of a trip from the southern U.S. to perform in Vermont, travelling through the Appalachians, through snowstorms and two-lane roads along the Appalachian Way. They were losing time and had to put their make-up on in the bus. "When we finally arrived, the whole audience was out on the street cheering us on." Audiences clearly wanted to support the fledgling company, even in its difficult moments. The theatre was old and they had to squeeze behind the stage, rubbing their white tutus on a dirty carpet, cleaning off the dirt with an old cloth. "We were just in time for our entrance and the performance continued—I had my very first slice of pizza that evening. Delicious!"

Lorna Geddes remembers how they entertained themselves on the long bus rides—one trip covered over 1200 miles in three days—and they were "pretty sick of the bus." But they sang, played geography games, twenty questions, and charades. Lorna also reports a near-disaster while driving for almost four hundred miles through a snowstorm over the Allegheny Mountains, again in the Appalachians. At one point the bus went into a ditch, but back out again. They arrived at nine p.m. for an eight-thirty performance. Most of the dancers were sick from the drive, and all of them laughed throughout the performance because they were hysterical. The next morning's review said it was worth every minute of the forty-five minute wait.

Lilian Jarvis considered it a luxury to ride on trains, rather than buses, across Canada and to Mexico. She appreciated the necessity of touring as a way to make ballet accessible to a "hockey-minded population." As well, it was necessary to augment insufficient government funding and box office receipts, which always kept the Company on the brink and dancers' livelihoods in question.

Frances Greenwood remembers mostly the "endless hours staring out of a bus window, the smell of damp tights and leotards, and the utter joy of being a member of an ever-evolving and changing community of artists, who put themselves on the line every time they stepped on a stage." One of the difficulties the dancers found in performing in so many different places was getting used to different stages. Some would be raked (sloped, rising away from the audience) and some would be waxed, rendered slippery and hazardous. At a Catholic school in Windsor, Ontario, an enthusiastic priest could not wait to tell them that the floor had been waxed to a "superior shine." On a Northern Ontario tour, more than once they found themselves dancing on temporary stages in hockey arenas "terrified of falling six feet to the ice below." From hockey arenas in Northern Ontario they moved to dancing outside in the Carter Barron Amphitheatre in Rock Creek Park, in Washington, DC, to a packed audience of four thousand, where they spotted important people in the audience such as Leonid Brezhnev, a future leader of the USSR. They also attended a reception in the elegant Canadian Embassy and had a photo shoot in the National Art Gallery.

Myrna Aaron reports that they danced in high school auditoriums or gymnasiums, sports arenas, old movie houses, and on the "rare occasion," with any luck, in actual theatres. The uncertain settings and capabilities of each theatre occasionally necessitated quick thinking. Frances Greenwood recalls one time when the soloists were dancing a most moving *pas-de-deux* in Swan Lake, scenery began to fall over onto the *corps de ballet* swans standing near the wings, where they would most certainly be hit on the head. "So, with great aplomb and the help of an offstage hand, we turned, raised our arms gracefully, and one, two, three gently set it upright before returning to our positions."Oldyna Dynowska recalls a stage-related disaster while touring, the kind that becomes funny in hindsight. "While touring, on one small stage during the Merliton dance from *The Nutcracker* we had a memorable mishap. Angela Leigh, who performed the chief Merliton, had lately been having a problem with her pirouettes, which was exacerbated by the close proximity on this small stage. She managed one shaky pirouette at the end, lost her balance, knocked over the two dancers behind her and so on, until all five dancers were flat on their backs, frilly crotches framed by their tutus toward the audience."

In Nashville, Tennessee, Lorna Geddess wrote a postcard to her parents and described a performance in a university gymnasium with no stage, no curtain, no wings, just a backdrop of thick white paper over wood frames to give some hiding. The bleachers along the side were full and the audience there only saw the sides and backs of the dancers while the audience on the floor was on the same level as the dancers, only two feet away from the show, with the orchestra off to one side. "But did they ever love it! The floor markings were helpful in keeping us in line."

Lorna Geddes also wrote to her parents, describing a performance at the University of South Dakota where the stage was very slippery as it was actually a basketball court. And in a wee town called Albert Lee they performed in a high school where the first six feet of the stage was like glass and the rest of the shallow stage was like Sauble Beach on Lake Huron— uneven, ripply, splinters all over—"ruined a new pair of pointe shoes—splinters stuck in them." These were their venues.

Frances Greenwood provides insight into a fundamental focus of the Company. "Despite the times we were sleep-deprived, hungry, injured, homesick, poor, under-appreciated or taken advantage of, I will always look at those years as my finishing school years: difficult, personally challenging, educating, and leaving wonderful memories. Whatever individual ambitions we as dancers had, we always seemed to pull up our socks and tights together to deliver the best performance we could at the time, because that audience on the other side of the curtain deserved it." Frances suggests that, "in a way we were the tools Celia needed to build the Company." Not only were they creating a ballet company, they were creating audiences across Canada and the United States "who had never seen a ballet before, nor heard the exquisite music." In a small southern American town, when they finished the performance, there was dead silence. Then the entire audience jumped to their feet and then gave them an uproarious applause that went on and on.

Bob Ito relates a story about performing in the Southern States in the dining hall of a Black college. The stage was rigged to accommodate the side-light and a student manned the spotlight. They performed *Les Sylphides*. The audience was absolutely mesmerized; it was the first ballet they had ever seen. When it ended there was complete silence, followed by thunderous applause. "We were invited to visit the famous Handy's Bar, but because of the segregation laws we were accompanied by the Sheriff." Frances adds, "We were establishing this wonderful ballet company that is now the jewel that Celia Franca envisioned and hoped for."

Food was often a problem while touring. While travelling through the Appalachians on one trip, they got lost and managed to find what seemed to be the only restaurant, owned and operated by an elderly couple. Bob Ito explains: "The service was too slow, so a couple of the girls offered to help and ended up doing all the cooking and the serving; we paid our bills and left the couple in a daze." When they were in Columbia, South Carolina, Lorna Geddes remembers that as there were fifteen hundred marines in town, mostly drunk by eleven p.m. when the dancers would be looking for food, Celia told them not to leave the hotel at all!

Brian Macdonald and Bob Ito in The Nutcracker Suite, *1952. Photo: Ballard and Jarrett. Courtesy: National Ballet Archives.*

More positively, in San Antonia Texas, in 1962, they were able to have a restaurant dinner after their show—huge steak, salad, baked potato, coffee, big slice of cheesecake—for $1.85.

Francis Greenwood was the roommate of Teresa Mann, a dancer a bit older than she. Teresa carried an electric frying pan with supplies in her suitcase. Cooking was not permitted in the hotel rooms, but if management knocked on the door Teresa took the frying pan and food into a closet or bathroom and sent naïve-looking Frances to the door where she would "lie through my teeth: No sir, there isn't anyone cooking here." Shirley Kash recalls ketchup soup. She and her friends would go to a restaurant, order a bowl of hot water, then add ketchup, salt, and pepper; they took the crackers and bread back to the hotel for later. Some of them also used immersion heaters to heat water in their hotel rooms for tea.

Judie Colpman's memories are of the times they would be invited to a person's home for a dinner after the performance. In Texas their hosts fed them "these incredible barbequed steaks." What was a bit tricky was that the hosts wanted to talk to the dancers, who were so "crazed with hunger" that they could not engage in conversation. Judie also reports that sometimes they would buy fruit and cheese, and sometimes baby food! It was usually easier to get late meals in Canada because the Chinese restaurants would be open late. "God bless 'em."

Bob Ito reports that when they returned from the tours, they would be met by members of the Ladies Auxiliary. "We looked haggard and undernourished. Some of the girls still had traces of wet white and dark eyeshadow from the last performance. The sight of us must have shocked the ladies because we were given Similac, a powdered milk formula for babies, and bottles of various vitamins to supplement our diet."

Lorna Geddes recalls staying in "this filthy old hotel" where the plumber told them their floor had been closed for four years. And it was the most expensive one on the tour, at twenty-one dollars per night, because there was a jewellers' convention in town. No TV, dirty, cockroaches everywhere; sometimes they slept on the floor because of cockroaches in the beds. The theatre in this town was not great either, but there was a reception at an inn where they stayed until two a.m. and where the food was edible. "There were hundreds of people, and a bar that sold sandwiches and as much salad as you could eat for forty-five cents."

These dancers made very little money. Still, sometimes while touring, the dancers would be asked to donate their change so the tour could continue, and everyone always gave whatever they could. The musicians, who were unionized, and the stagehands, who made a higher salary than Celia, refused to donate. Lilian Jarvis explains that although competition and rivalry existed within the Company and the dancers were in it for themselves, it was never at the expense of the Company. "When we were each asked at least once if not twice to forego our week's salary for the sake of the Company there was not a dissenting voice. Loyalty to the cause was expected and for the most part freely given."

Lilian explains how they managed when not touring. The lucky ones had family in Toronto; others shared accommodations on their twenty-five-dollar-a-week salaries. And these salaries were only from September to June. Summer jobs were whatever one could get. Some men worked lifting boxes in a shipping room; "Earl Kraul liked this as it developed his strength for lifting his partners." Some got dancing jobs at the Exhibition or Dufferin Mall's Melody Fair theatre-in-the-round. But in spite of making so little money, Lilian says that it was thrilling to be in the Company in those years when even the Bolshoi and American Ballet Russes were attended only by ballet aficionados. It was exciting beyond belief to be on the ground floor of a homegrown company. "A treasured privilege."

Donald Mahler provides perhaps one of the most beautiful memories, shared by so many others. "Those early years were scenes of hard work and sometimes privation. The pay was minimal, but the rewards were great. What we had was the great satisfaction of knowing that we were sharing in the creation of something very important. Additionally, we had the opportunity to dance, dance, and dance. They were years for which I will always be grateful. For friendships and shared times both good and not so good, and for a life in Art, thank you National Ballet of Canada. And to my beloved Celia—I will always love you for your help and belief in me. No thanks would be adequate!"

Finally, Yves Cousineau leaves a lasting memory. "We are the ones who are still alive to talk about the National Ballet of Canada during the fifties. We are very proud of it and very humbled by the experience. We were the first stones that built that magnificent Company. Yes, the fifties were indeed the pioneering years. Most of us came from across Canada and we were happy and excited to be selected to participate in this new Ballet Company.... We were all on the same buses, awakening audiences to Canadian ballet. And I believe that we had some splendid performances, even in those hockey arenas of Ontario and elsewhere. Most of the time one could feel a warm bond among all of the dancers. We were the adventurers of the 1950s, lacking nothing in soul and trying to maintain ourselves with our aches, pains, and some dreams."

Myrna Aaron. Courtesy: National Ballet Archives

6.
In Their Own Words

THE MATERIAL I RECEIVED from my fellow dancers was rich in anecdotes, shared experiences, and interesting points of view. While I wove many of these stories into this narrative of the early years of the Company, it was impossible to find a suitable place for them all. Not wanting to deprive you, the reader, I have here included additional memorable (or at least notable) stories from several of the dancers' accounts that didn't quite fit elsewhere.

MYRNA AARON

Although as of this writing, it has been sixty-seven years since I saw Celia Franca for the first time, the memory is as vivid as if it happened yesterday. She had just completed her cross-Canada journey to see if there were dancers enough to form a potential ballet company. She was back in Toronto, working in the box office at Eaton Auditorium to support herself. On Sunday mornings, she taught a two-hour class at Boris Volkoff's studio on Yonge Street. Those of us who had been chosen to attend were so excited that first day, and of course dying to be chosen for the new Company. Most of us were local, but Earl Kraul and Colleen Kenney came from Hamilton every week, and I expect there were others who travelled long ways to be there.

Those were great days. We worked under awful circumstances for almost no money and loved every minute. Celia often told us how spoiled we were—she after all, had performed in London while German bombs were falling. I'm grateful to have been a

Edelayne Brandt and Diane Childenhaus in Offenbach in the Underworld.
Courtesy. Private collection.

dancer back then. It was a very special time that dancers today with their sprung floors and company massage therapists don't get to experience.

VICTORIA BERTRAM

I had just graduated from the National Ballet School the spring before. Not having passed the "ideal perfect dancer's body" assessment, Miss Oliphant deemed me a good candidate for the teacher's training course and so I was to stay on in this capacity. How very surprised I was then, when I received a phone call from none other than Miss Celia Franca to replace one of the dancers (Cathy Carr) who had been sidelined by an injury. So there I was, bounding up that old staircase to report for my first day of rehearsal!

At the end of the four-week tour ... I went back to school assuming I had only been hired for that tour. A day or so later I got a telephone call. It was Miss Franca once again, this time asking me where on earth I was! "Get back here," she said. "We need you!"

GLORIA BONNELL

I must confess I loved dancing in *Winter Night,* and I loved it even more for the fact that we were not required to wear pointe shoes. It was heavenly to give those toes a rest! I don't recall disliking any of our ballets. I think I loved them all, but perhaps memory fails me now—this was, after all, over fifty years ago!

It was about 1959, during Celia Franca's final performance of *Giselle.* It was also my last performance as I, a member of the *corps de ballet,* was leaving the Company. The memory of tears streaming down both my and Miss Franca's faces, is vivid all of these decades later. Along with the emotion at that time, I have always felt so blessed to have shared that amazing experience with such an icon of the Canadian ballet world.

EDELAYNE BRANDT

I was in awe of Celia Franca, both as a gifted dancer and as our leader. She demanded professionalism at all times. One slip and you would hear about it. Miami Beach comes to mind. A few of us were sent to the famous beach for a publicity photo shoot [for *Swan Lake*]. Being young and knowing it was snowing back in Toronto, we stayed to frolic on the sand. Miss Franca took one look at our neon sunburns and scathingly told us we "looked more like flamingos than swans!"

Being an unknown Canadian company, our audiences in small American cities could be sparse; that was when pranks would break out. One night down South, Miss Franca was dancing

Swanhilda [in *Coppelia*] to a house of no more than thirty people. When she flung open the drape to reveal Coppelia [a life-sized doll], there sat David Haber [the company stage manager] in full doll costume with wig in place, batting long false eyelashes. Franca let out a small yelp but, being a consummate professional, held it all together. Everyone else onstage lost it, even though we knew a stern lecture would follow—and it did!

SALLY BRAYLEY

My goal was to dance with the National Ballet of Canada. So, after the New Year of 1956 I moved to Toronto to study with Betty Oliphant. At the time I arrived, I went to class every day with Betty. The students were all younger than me, but I didn't care; I was determined to dance with the Company. During this phase of training, Celia often came and watched the class I was in. After six months of hard work and just before the start of the annual summer school, lo and behold Celia asked me to join the Company. This was my dream come true.

There were so many funny experiences during my six seasons with the National Ballet of Canada, some sad, some bad, but all experiences I carry with me to this day. These memories are the backbone of what I have done and not done throughout my career as a dancer, director, teacher, coach, administrator, fundraiser, and my overall life and career in the great world of dance. I am still friends with many of the dancers and people who were part of the National Ballet of Canada during those first ten years. I am so proud and honoured to have been part of that time when we were making Canadian dance history.

CATHY CARR

I remember after dancing four acts of *Swan Lake* in Montreal and meeting some friends of mine from McGill University afterwards, I allowed myself only a bran muffin and a fruit cup to make sure that I did not gain a sliver. This was an example of the perils of body image. Weight gain was front and centre at all times. To this day, I live with an eating disorder and being underweight is

Sally Brayley in Coppelia. *Photo: Ken Bell. Courtesy: National Ballet Archives.*

the operative ideal. Recently, I completed my grade eight piano exam, and my grade seven theory exam. I love yoga, tennis, walking, and opera. I still love to dance and music is very central to my life.

Being part of the National Ballet Company was a unique experience and I will never regret my decision to become a dancer at such a young age. Notwithstanding, I missed many of the normal stages of development, some of life's adventures went missing, and undoubtedly this left some scars. However, I will never forget the experiences gained and the opportunities I had brushing up against such talented artists.

Marcel Chojnacki, Lilian Jarvis, and Earl Kraul in Coppelia, *1958. Photo: Ken Bell.
Courtesy: National Ballet Archives.*

MARCEL CHOJNACKI

One favourite ballet was *Coppelia,* where Celia Franca and I performed the lead roles. Celia performed Swanhilda, the village girl dressed as a doll come to life, and I performed Dr. Coppelius. This role was both interesting and complex; it involved considerable mime, interpretation, and exacting dance choreography in conjunction with the music. After performing in that role for some time, I switched roles and danced the czardas in *Coppelia.*

In Mexico City, one of the dancers scheduled to perform the czardas in Swan Lake became ill. I was asked if I knew the choreography and if I would be able to dance it. Indeed I did; I made it a practice to learn the repertoire of every ballet we performed. I used my knowledge of dance repertoire during my years working as a ballet master, choreographer, and dancer with Les Feux Follets, the National Dance Ensemble and Les Sortileges in Montreal throughout the 1960s and beyond.

JUDIE COLPMAN

Oldyna Dynowska was a friend from my earliest classes with Bettina Byers, a well-known teacher of the Royal Academy of Dance in Toronto. Oldyna and I attended the National Ballet Summer School at the same time, both of us hoping to audition for the new Company, although I had a feeling Oldyna had already been approached to join. At the end of the summer school, Miss Franca pulled me aside and told me that she was not inviting me to join the Company. After another year of hard work, I should audition again. I was crushed, but I knew that I had to forge ahead with my technique and try again next year. Yes, I would do just that.

Two days later, Franca's office contacted me to pick up a pair of red boots from Oldyna and bring them back to the University of Toronto's Varsity Stadium that night before the performance of *Coppelia* Act II, which she and a small group of dancers were presenting as part of a summer festival of music and dance. With no expectations, I took the boots backstage to Miss

Franca's dressing room. She thanked me for the boots and, to my complete surprise, asked me to join the new National Ballet Company she was creating. I said yes and that was that! She told me to watch for an invitation to a first party at her home where people would get together to meet the dancers and staff of the new National Ballet of Canada. What had just happened? I could hardly believe this amazing invitation to become a professional dancer!

YVES COUSINEAU

I wish to write about another student who was taking classes at the time I was studying with Elizabeth Leese. The National Ballet was performing at the National Arts Center in Ottawa before we were to leave for the World Fair in Osaka [in 1970]. A few of us were invited to have lunch at the Parliament buildings. We were introduced to Pierre Elliot Trudeau. When he introduced himself to me, he said, "But I know you, we studied in the same studio."

I said, "But I don't remember you being in my class."

He said "You would not. I was in the class for stupid adults." Dear Pierre.

We were all under Celia's scrutiny, especially the girls. There were some members who became depressed and upset by the stress of training. Touring so long at a time, we would encounter many problems along the way. This living, travelling, and performing with so many people and for so many weeks could really get under your skin. Celia's constant supervision and corrections immediately after the performance upset many of us. We were not all professional dancers, and many of us had much to learn, and many things at the same time. In those days, schools and academies for dance did not exist in the same way they do today. Dancers learned on the go; you either endured the corrections and prevailed, or left.

Then came Antony Tudor to choreograph *Offenbach in the Underworld* for the Company. I was given the role of a waiter, but most fascinating was hearing this master speak about the process whereby he invented every character to be played and danced. He spoke plainly about the details of movements and their meaning—sometimes in very graphic details. The ballet's setting was a cabaret in the Underworld. He explained to everyone the night life of this café—its nightly intrigue and the kind of girls the can-can girls were. He was real and direct. He was the first person I had met in the dance world who gave proper directions. He was a creator, a director, a choreographer. Though I was dancing a small role, for the first time I was directed artistically. During my time studying the dramatic arts, I soon learned that there are no small roles, just small actors.

OLDYNA DYNOWSKA

Many years ago I read *Theatre Street* by Karsavina. I greatly admired the Russian dancer, Ulanova. She was modest in demeanour and did not have the ideal physique for a dancer, but when she danced, she created the most moving visions and feelings that went beyond the mere physical movements of the choreography. Years later, I read a poem by John Masefield called, "The Dauber" in which he described this wonderful phenomenon as "turning water into wine." Even though Masefield had been describing the painter's absorption in his art, that metaphor described how I saw the art of dancing.

It is possible that some see the evolution of the National Ballet Company as a continuum; however, this model does not consider or appreciate the many aspects of the sacrifices, the dedication, and the perseverance of those first dancers, and of the hardworking champions of those first years, all of whom laid a foundation for the possibility of a Canadian ballet. The correct model to my mind is a vertical construction, which shows the present Company as standing firmly on the shoulders and the sacrifices of those first dancers, and of the many unsung others who contributed to the first struggling but persevering building blocks of the National Ballet of Canada.

KATRINA EVANOVA

Once Patricia Neary and I passed our examination, achieving a "highly recommended" mark in the Cecchetti Syllabus, Celia

Oldyna Dynowska. Photo: Maurice Seymour Studios.
Courtesy: Private collection.

Franca contracted us to join the National Ballet Company early in 1957. No words could express the jubilation we experienced. I wasn't yet seventeen! It was popular to adopt a stage name if yours didn't sound appealing. I simply extended my nickname, Katie, to "Katrina" and used the feminine version of my Bulgarian surname, "Evanova."

After a night's performance, being awakened at five-thirty in the morning by a desk clerk, having had less than five hours of sleep, was enough to make anyone grumpy, but I tried to maintain a friendly, cheerful manner. Hurrying to be presentable, packing, paying the hotel bill, and scarfing down a quick breakfast in time to catch the next bus was always draining. Once on board, I'd flop into my seat, pull out my corduroy neck rest, and nap. We always had our main meal after performances. By the time we returned to our room, showered, and washed a few articles, it was past midnight. Life was analogous to being in the army. We'd mount the bus, lugging a book, transistor radio, and Kodak camera.

LORNA GEDDES

Miss Franca was a taskmaster, but she had reason to be. It was necessary to be strict, necessary for us to learn an awful lot, and this was the woman who had all the theatrical knowledge that we needed. She was funny. She challenged us. And we did our very best to meet that challenge because she was also a little bit frightening. Certainly I think a little bit of fear is good; it will allow you to never give in and she wouldn't let you. She always wanted the best out of you. But she did appreciate it. And we knew we were progressing.

The touring. One-night stands. Down to Texas and back through the South. I loved it. I loved it because I was being paid to do what I wanted to do, which was dance, and I was travelling and I was seeing the world and I was taking pictures. And there was so much to learn.

I think my first contract was forty-two dollars per week. And the first year I made eleven hundred dollars because we were only hired for seven months and then we had five months off at seventeen dollars per week unemployment insurance. I do have

Janet Green (Foster), 1959. Photo: Ken Bell. Courtesy: National Ballet Archives

my income tax forms and I think the poverty level at that time for two people living together was four thousand dollars so we were below that (Tennant, *The Dancers' Story*).

JANET GREEN FOSTER

Students came to the Elmhurst Ballet School in Camberly, England, from all over the world. The school offered the full

British academic curriculum as well as theatrical and ballet training. Juliet and Haley Mills were acting students, and it was high excitement when their famous father, John Mills, came to the school performances. But for the large group of us who enrolled mainly for ballet, the formal "education" was not exactly academic. Classes were held around the dining room table and our "schooling" consisted of the History of Ballet, the History of Music, English Composition, Conversational French, and Current Affairs. The latter class was the liveliest, especially when the Hungarian Revolution and Suez Crisis erupted the following year. But if the "academics" offered little by way of formal education, they gave us many more hours in the day to dance.

Whenever CBC needed dancers, they turned to the National and when the Company was not touring I danced on television shows. Little did I know that the friends and contacts I was making within the CBC would lead me smoothly and quickly into television production upon leaving the ballet world. Looking back over the two years I danced with the National, it is the touring I remember most: the one-night stands, travelling by bus from one city to another, hoping there would be time for Shirley Kash to give us class onstage before the performance, wondering what the theatre and stage would be like. I carried a Kodak Pony IV camera and took every chance to explore the cities and countryside we passed through: the wild and more natural landscapes of North Ontario, the Maritimes, Florida, Texas, and the New Orleans of the times. For the first time, I was becoming aware of a much wider world. And there were many other influences, outside the ballet, pulling me steadily in a different direction.

FRANCES GREENWOOD

Touring was very taxing and wore out the body and soul. Because we were always sharing such close quarters, colds and flu were constantly passed from person to person. One year, so many members of the *corps de ballet* were too ill to perform that even when all the soloists were substituted we were still short one dancer. It was *Swan Lake* and I was the smallest dancer

From left to right: Diane Ireland, Frances Greenwood, Betty Pope, Katrina Evanova, and Cathy Carr. Courtesy: National Ballet Archives.

so I was made to dance the lead swan while Celia, subbing in, decided it would be best if she were behind me. She got through it wonderfully, but there was a lot of whispering under my breath and the audience probably thought I was talking to myself!

Just before we were to leave on my first tour in the fall of 1956, Celia called me into her office for a chat. "Frances, darling," she began, "your name, Frances Greenbaum, is not in the programmes for the season. I don't know if you are familiar with the British movie star, Joan Greenwood, but I thought it best to change your name to Frances Greenwood. That is your new stage name. I think you should go home and tell your parents." Of course, my family was furious at my not being consulted or asked if I wanted my new stage name. Many years later, I read that Celia's name was originally Celia Franks, but Dame Ninette de Valois changed it to Franca. I wonder if she was asked or if it was just done.

Many difficult life lessons were learned while touring through the United States. Our American manager had to explain to us that we were not to enter washrooms, areas of restaurants, or sit on bus seats with signs that read "for coloured persons only."

One time we were in Houston, Texas, and were invited to the Houston Cattlemen's Club for a very swank reception after our performance. As we arrived at the venue, Celia came up to me and whispered, "Frances, dear, don't let anyone know that you are Jewish." The club was restricted and did not allow people of colour or Jews. That was not the only time that life's ugliness reared its head.

BOB ITO

One memorable event comes to mind: our invitation to the Russian Embassy in Washington, DC, to screen a documentary about the Bolshoi; our first taste of Russian caviar and vodka.

Another memory from an American tour was our first encounter with Los Angeles. While travelling to Glendale, orange orchards lined the freeway and the smell of orange blossoms was overpowering. I remember Galveston, Texas, where we took our shoes off and waded into the warm waters of the Gulf of Mexico. And going up the east coast of Florida, we parked on Daytona Beach and all went for a swim. Unfortunately, our driver was docked for it, because the stop was not on the itinerary.

One grievance while on tour in small towns was that all of the restaurants were closed by the time we finished our performance. The receptions we would attend only offered cake and cookies, and most dancers had not had much to eat before the performance. We posted a petition and the following performances were followed with substantial meals. We also scavenged fruit and rolls and any goodies we could slip into our "dance bag."

While I was with the Company I had the opportunity to work on television. Brian Macdonald was choreographer in the weekly variety show *Tourbillion* in Montreal. So many of the National Ballet dancers were able to work during the summer break. After leaving the National Ballet, I followed the opportunities that came my way. I continued to work on television with Allan

Lilian Jarvis as the White Girl in Winter Night. *Courtesy: National Ballet Archives.*

Lund for the programs *Mr Show Business, The Shirley Harmer Show, Hit Parade, The Robert Gould and Joan Sullivan Show,* and occasionally *The Wayne and Shuster Show*, with Don Gilles.

LILIAN JARVIS

Because of my body structure, ballet technique did not really "work" for me. My preference for roles therefore leaned strongly to the lyrical and storyline ballets, where technique was not so critical. I danced many of the early ballets, like Grant Strate's *Ballad* and Franca's *Le Pommier,* with a sense of ease and enjoyment. These ballets were also well-suited to the male segment of our audiences, who were as yet uncomfortable seeing male dancers in tights. And to be sure, as we peeked through the curtain in those early years to get a reading on our audience before performances, a male presence was rare.

Interesting, again because of their musical precision, I loved dancing the "Machine Girl" in David Adams' early *Ballet Behind Us*, with its staccato movements, and Balanchine's meticulously choreographed *Concerto Borocco* and his beauty-to-dance *Serenade.* Another gem for me was the Spanish dance in Coppelia. With its musicality and vitality still lingering in my bones, it's the only dance I can reproduce from memory to this day. How ephemeral is the life of a dancer!

Of course, my greatest moment came when I danced Juliet at the special matinee performance of *Romeo and Juliet* for the Company's twenty-fifth anniversary celebration. The ballet came into the repertoire the year after I left to study in New York and I had dearly regretted having missed the opportunity to dance that most prized dramatic role. And so, when I had the unexpected opportunity at the age of forty-five to enact that heart-achingly beautiful role, with its lush choreography and stirring music by Prokofiev, my aspirations for a dance life were satisfied to the greatest extent that was possible.

SHIRLEY KASH

I loved character dance, which I felt was in my DNA. In those early years, immigrants from Poland, Ukraine, Russia, and Hungary would have a picnic at Pickering. We all dressed in our national costumes, sampled traditional cuisines, and performed our dances and music—an amazing cultural experience.

I had wonderful teacher training and mentorship from Betty Oliphant from twelve to sixteen years of age. At sixteen, I got into the National Ballet. Betty opened a satellite school in Willowdale and I taught there. That's where Vanessa Harwood first took lessons. Betty founded a line of five dancers who performed at the Royal York ballroom. It was a tap line, but they also did the can-can. Betty choreographed everything and I was part of this line.

I loved teaching so much that I finally chose to leave the Company to join the faculty at the newly founded National Ballet School. My teaching gave me great joy and it is a privilege to have been part of the lives of those who went on to have great dance careers.

VALERIE LYON

One of my memories was when I watched with awe as Lois Smith injured her side but was quickly injected by a local doctor to kill the pain before she proceeded to perform anyway to everyone's amazement and trepidation. I had the utmost respect and admiration for Lois Smith, especially as Swan Queen. My favourite ballets were the classics: *Swan Lake* (especially Celia's version after Petipa), *Les Sylphides*, and *Giselle*. I loved dancing in the *corps* of these ballets. I remember fondly dancing in the Norman Campbell-directed *Swan Lake* for television. I wholeheartedly disliked modern works, especially *The Remarkable Rocket,* and was only forced to dance in this ballet once when someone was injured, with only a day's notice.

In 1961, I stopped dancing of my own volition to become a Novitiate of the Ministry of the Little Flower of Jesus. I did a four-year novitiate and eventually became Prioress of the monastery. While I stopped dancing cold turkey, and missed the exercise, I found the strengths gained in dancing were eminently transferrable to my new life.

Donald Mahler. Courtesy: National Ballet Archives.

DONALD MAHLER

I fell in love with the members of the Company. Not only did they do many of the great classics, but they had four of Mr. [Antony] Tudor's masterpieces. In addition, their training was based on the very same Cecchetti syllabus that I had been training for under Miss [Margaret] Craske [at the Metropolitan Opera House]. The next time the Company came to New York, I asked Mr. Tudor if he could arrange for me to take class with them. I duly appeared at the theater onstage. The class was taught by Betty Oliphant. At the barre, she came up behind me and said, "Can't you keep your hips straight?" With a devilish smile I said, "No." That should have been the end of me, but the next day during Mr. Tudor's class at the Met, he came over to me at the barre and said, with a twinkle in his eye, "Can't you keep your hips straight?" Some telephone conversations must have occurred!

In any case, I was invited to come to Toronto to attend that year's summer school with a view to entering the Company in the fall. As luck would have it, the Company was engaged to appear in Washington, DC, and I received notice to come to Toronto immediately to replace a dancer who had been let go. No sooner had I arrived when that dancer was rehired. Now they had me as well and the roster was expanded by one.

I was given my first role, a mouse in *The Nutcracker*. My first performance was a disaster due to the darkness onstage and the masks we all had to wear. I couldn't recognize anybody or see where I was going and so I missed my first entrance, ran over to the other side of the stage, having to cross over under the stage, only to find that my fellow mice had made the second entrance without me. And so I never actually made it on the stage and my debut was as a non-existent mouse!

We all used to don various items of clothing to keep warm during class. Hockey socks were all the rage. We wore sweaters and sometimes even overcoats.

PAULINE MCCULLAGH

My debut with the Company was delayed because of a broken foot. "What happened to you?" asked a perturbed Betty Oliphant when I hobbled into rehearsal. "I fell off the streetcar," was the embarrassed answer. After several months in a cast and then physiotherapy in a swimming pool, I returned to classes and rehearsals.

Shirley Kash patiently taught us our roles, we darned our pointe shoes, and Celia Franca smoked endlessly. In trains we did ballet barre, holding the securing railings in the corridor. At the outdoor Carter Barron Amphitheatre in Washington, we were

Betty Pope, Lilian Jarvis, Angela Leigh, and Lois Smith wearing hockey stockings, c. 1957.
Courtesy: Lois Smith Electronic Archives at Dance Collection Danse.

accompanied on stage once by a huge moth and once by a small, frantic dog.

On my own initiative, I understudied *Dark Elegies*. Then a dancer was injured and I replaced her at the last minute. But the best part was the great David Adams thanking me afterwards. I loved dancing Brian Macdonald's fun choreography on television. Just before she left the Company, a pregnant dancer asked to take my place in *Offenbach*. She wanted one last kick at the can-can.

I did not get to really know Miss Franca until fifty years afterwards, shortly before her death, when I used to visit her in the retirement residence. By then, I had also read her biography. One day, her ballet-distorted feet peeking out from the end of her bed, free of the pressure of sheets, she surprised me by asking, "Are you happy?"

Pauline McCullagh, 1956. Courtesy: Private collection.

CECILY PAIGE

I cannot remember a time when I did not want to dance, even though classes were not available due to the War. At the time, though, I had no idea what ballet meant.

I had an offer from Franca to join her in Canada. This was a wonderful experience with supportive dancers. Touring was exhausting, but I was able to dance night-in and night-out!

My favourite ballet is and always will be *Giselle*. I first danced it in the *corps* at Sadler's Wells. In Canada, I truly enjoyed *Le*

Carnival, with Bob Ito, a very gallant partner. *Winter Night—*
poor Mary, whose hands must have been falling off playing Rach
II on a regular basis. *Offenbach in the Underworld*—what fun!

Lilian was the most delightful Swanhilda. I have seen many
over the years, but her sweetness and delightful performance in
Coppelia was hard to match. I also admired Jackie Ivings' work
and Bev Banfield's acting, especially in *Nutcracker*.

MARILYN ROLLO

These first months of classes and rehearsals were very difficult,
not only for the dancers, but also for Celia Franca who had to
train and work with all of us and try to turn us into professional
ballet dancers. Miss Franca was a taskmaster. Personally, I was
terrified of her, and that feeling stayed with me for many years.

There are lots of other memories, becoming friends with so
many people that I still have contact with today. This whole
experience is something one could never simply forget. You are a
close-knit bunch, together for so many hours per day.

Just recalling all these memories has brought back many more.

PENELOPE ANNE WINTER

Celia Franca wore a thick black braid that swung down to
her *derrière*. By the end of class, we would see a new side of
Miss Franca. She would morph into *Sleeping Beauty*'s witch,
Carabosse, her black, unruly hair covering most of her face and
petite torso.

The Company was in its sixth year when I joined in 1956. Thus
began the emotional and physical tsunami of being in a fledging
ballet company just getting its sea legs while I was still just a
youngster myself. We depended on kind donations from strangers
and attempted to educate ourselves at every opportunity.

A fifty-year memorial coin is still proudly displayed on my
mementos shelf. Nearby is an autographed glossy of Celia kicking
up her oh-so-gnarled toes in *Offenbach in the Underworld,*
which was autographed and gifted to me by Celia for being
the "best cygnet" in a school performance [of *Swan Lake*] the

Jocelyn Terell and Jacqueline Ivings in Concerto Barocco, *1961. Photo: Ken Bell. Courtesy: National Ballet Archives*

year I joined the National Ballet. In Hamilton, preparing for *Giselle,* I recall Celia begging us to keep our weight well over our feet in an attempt to stay grounded. In the second act, I was conscious of her bidding, and was horrified to hear a terrible crash. Saddened to think of the poor dancer who had fallen I realized that it was my own chin on the floor. By the end of that tour, having achieved more noteworthy roles, I silently renamed myself Penelope Fall!

LEILA ZORINA

Here are a few memories from those long-ago tours. The first tour in Mexico City when so many dancers were ill, Miss Franca replaced the girl in front of me in the *corps* in *Lac 2.* I prompted her through the performance. Another time, I had to replace

Penny Winter in *The Remarkable Rocket* without a rehearsal; She was in the wings prompting me.

In Texas one year, after a performance they opened up the Officers' Club for us as the restaurants were closed. A gentleman asked me to dance and I did. When I came back to the table I was told by the other dancers that if I danced with him again we would all be thrown out. I had not known that a white person was not supposed to dance with a black gentleman.

Other memories are of dancing on stages in very, very cold hockey arenas. And the day that Patty and I jumped out of bed thinking that we were late for the bus. When we arrived in the lobby there was no one there. It was the middle of the night.

Norman Campbell and Celia Franca on the set of Swan Lake *for CBC.*
Courtesy: York University Libraries, Clara Thomas Archives and Special Collections,
Robert Lawson fonds, ASC04651.

7.
EARLY CHAMPIONS

SADLY, MANY PEOPLE IMPORTANT to those early years of the National Ballet have died. This is not surprising, as it was so long ago, but their memories live on in the minds of those whose lives they touched. We are very grateful to them, and they should be remembered. To that end, I contacted several other luminaries from the dance community today to ask them to write a tribute to these champions of the past.

CELIA FRANCA EARLY YEARS

CELIA FRANCA WAS BORN CELIA FRANKS in 1921 in London, daughter of Polish immigrants. She began her study of dance at the age of four, studying at the Guildhall School of Music and the Royal Academy of Dance, as well as with Stanislas Idzikowski, the Polish ballet master; Judith Espinoza, the renowned dance teacher; and the English choreographer Antony Tudor. She joined the Ballet Rambert in 1936, and made her professional debut there at age fifteen, choreographing her first piece in 1939. In 1941, at age twenty, she danced and choreographed for the Sadler's Wells Ballet and in 1947 became the ballet mistress of the Metropolitan Ballet. At this time, she began choreographing for television, creating *Eve of St. Agnes* and *Dance of Salome* for BBC. When Stewart James came to England in 1950, on behalf of a Toronto group who thought Canada was ready for a national ballet company, he met with Dame Ninette deValois, the Artistic Director of the Sadler's Wells Ballet. deValois recommended Celia Franca because of her many and varied

Marcel Chojnacki and Celia Franca in Coppelia, 1951. Photo: Kenneth J. Smith. Courtesy: National Ballet Archives.

strengths. deValois reportedly said that Franca was the greatest dramatic dancer the Wells ever had. At that time, Franca had been working in the world of ballet in London for fifteen years. In addition to her skills, she also had a network of contacts with dancers throughout Europe. Therefore, when developing her own company in Canada, she was able to invite them to perform. By the 1960s and 1970s, Franca was able to have stars such as Erik Bruhn and Rudolf Nureyev perform classical works for the National Ballet.

When she arrived in Toronto in 1950, the first thing Franca did was tour across the country to search for dancers. And she found them in various dance studios and community halls. Like Franca's Polish parents, in many cases the parents of these up-and-coming dancers had emigrated from other parts of the world and brought their culture with them, and all cultures include music and dance. Some of Franca's recruits came from the Polish and Ukrainian halls in Toronto. Others had been taking dancing lessons at the Boris Volkoff Studio. Some families were willing to move to accommodate their young child's desire to dance and were willing to allow and enable them to join this unknown life, touring across North America for very little money. Some young men were themselves immigrants and determined to join the world of ballet. What trust they must have put in Celia Franca. In some ways, she must have seemed like the Pied Piper of Hamelin. But Franca had more than just a magic pipe.

She was elegantly attractive with her dark, kohl-lined eyes, swept-back black hair, and stylish wardrobe. She could dance, teach, direct, and choreograph. She could fundraise and work with a board of directors as well as supporters. With her dancers, she was strict and demanded nothing but the best. She could be cruel to a struggling dancer, and very kind with her praise and encouragement to another, both critical and supportive. She could pick out the dancers with leading ballerina potential, and those who were strong members of the *corps*. There was no question that she was in charge, but she knew when to give way, such as when one dancer was fired because he could not be available for a particular tour. The rest of the Company objected, and she hired him back.

Celia's dancers saw what she was accomplishing in creating the National Ballet of Canada, and they recognized the gifts she gave to each of them personally. Bob Ito describes it as follows: "Looking back, I'm so grateful to Celia Franca for the opportunity she gave me, with her support and encouragement. She launched me into a career that I have enjoyed and prospered in. The many disciplines I learned in the ballet company have stayed with me. Thanks, Miss Franca."

—Jocelyn Terell

CELIA FRANCA LATER YEARS

THERE IS ONE WORD THAT penetrates the extraordinary fabric of myth and fact that clothes the memory of Celia Franca: "redoubtable." This means awe-inspiring, formidable, daunting, impressive, indomitable, fearsome, invincible, doughty, and alarming. By 1971, I was writing about dance just as the National Ballet Company really started coming into its own as a front-rank artistic endeavour in Canada. Its dancers were winning international competitions; its productions were being reviewed by *The New York Times*. Famous figures in the dance world, like Erik Bruhn and Rudolf Nureyev, were keen to sign on for guest appearances or to direct full-length productions. It was a golden era, especially for Celia Franca, who had fought for this moment with every ounce of her being.

It was impossible not to admire the struggle and tempestuous spirit that sustained her. She was a classic founding figure who didn't brook much opposition, who was used to setbacks and picking herself up again, who could defend her turf like a modern-day Boadicea, and who kept the goal of a national troupe worthy of international approbation and support in front of her at all time. As critics and board members alike would always eventually discover, Franca was indomitable and formidable. I once remember talking to a former National Ballet Board Chair, Senator Jack Godfrey. I asked him how he enjoyed his period at the constitutional helm working with the artistic director. He just looked at me with wild eyes. "Enjoy?" he asked me, almost incredulously. "Enjoy? That's not the word I would use. 'Survive' is the word I would use."

—John Fraser

KAY AMBROSE

KAY AMBROSE HAD WORKED with Celia Franca in England and came to Canada to help her establish her new ballet company. She was vital to the development of the National Ballet of Canada in its early years. Between 1951 and 1961 she designed sets and costumes for thirty productions including *Coppelia* and *Swan Lake.*

Originally known as the author of *The Ballet Lover's Companion* and *The Ballet Lover's Pocket-book,* Ambrose had expertise in classical ballet, as well as in Indian dance, from working for years with the Rom Gopal Dance Company in India. She sewed clothes, designed sets, and almost anything else the

Oldyna Dynowska and Kay Ambrose, 1952.
Courtesy: Myrna Aaron Electronic Archives at Dance Collection Danse.

dancers needed or wanted. According to Katrina Evanova, during a break in a performance she developed a nosebleed. "A passerby, the illustrious Kay Ambrose, acting as a nursemaid, ordered me to lay down on the concrete floor, and began pinching my nose in the appropriate area. I was grateful to her." Donald Mahler reiterates, "Celia and the Company really depended on her. She did everything for the dancers."

Ambrose always carried with her a sketchbook, including to hockey games and wrestling matches, where she was fascinated by the way people move. She was inspired by the early dancers and choreographers with the growing Company, believing they had the potential to become of international excellence. Speaking

Betty Oliphant, 1980.
Courtesy: National Ballet Archives.

Betty Oliphant, 1980.
Courtesy: National Ballet Archives.

of the Company in the *Los Angeles Times* in 1958, Ambrose recalled, "They have what Canada has, and it jumps out at you the moment the curtain goes up. I think it is vitality."

—Jocelyn Terell

BETTY OLIPHANT

I CAME TO CANADA FROM ENGLAND in 1951, when I was four years old. Celia Franca, also from England, had arrived in Canada just a few months prior to start the National Ballet of Canada. Franca needed a ballet mistress for the Company and chose Betty Oliphant. Miss O., as we called her, was also from England and arrived in Canada with her Canadian husband and two children.

When I was six years old my mother, who had danced ballet in England, decided that Miss O. was the best teacher in Toronto and that I should study dance with her. It also helped that we lived in Willowdale and Miss O. had a Saturday class in the North York Community Centre nearby. Truth be told, I didn't much like giving up my playtime on Saturdays, but I continued anyway. After a year, Miss O. suggested that I take classes in her "real" studio at 444 Sherbourne Street in downtown Toronto. That's where the like-minded students were, she told me. The studio, which was actually on the main floor of her house, had real dancer barres, not chairs, plus mirrors and a piano accompanist named Mrs. Mahew, and of course, Butterscotch, the cat, who weaved between our feet as we practiced our steps.

It is at Miss O.'s studio that I first met and studied with Nadia Potts, Veronica Tennant, Linda Fletcher, Vicki Bertram, Michele Starbuck, and Barbara Malinowski. But for Michele, all of us went on to join the National Ballet Company. Miss O.'s excellent assistants, especially Nancy Schwenker, also helped us immensely on our journey to become dancers. By this time Miss O. was a single mother of daughters, one of whom also took ballet lessons. The house was like my second home.

Miss O. introduced us to the National Ballet by taking all of us to the Royal Alexandra Theatre. We would watch from the second balcony for fifty cents. Each time the lights would dim, the music would start, and the curtain would rise on this magical land of beautiful dancers and costumes. After one particular performance of *Swan Lake,* Miss O. took us backstage to meet Lois Smith and David Adams. There Lois was, in her white tutu so wide it grazed both sides of the hallway. Right then I knew that she was all I wanted to be—the Swan Queen. And so it was that I danced *Swan Lake* as my first full-length ballet with the Company in 1972.

Classes continued, but now we were die-hard fans of the Company's dancers. The costumes for the ballets were stored in a room in the basement of Miss O.'s studio where we all got changed for class. We would, of course, try them on, imagining what it might be like to dance in them on stage. Naughty, maybe, but so much fun. In those days, Miss O. would call Barbara, Michele, and I "the Three Brats." Depending on who was in favour at the time she would rearrange our names. The first coup came when Barbara was chosen to dance Clara in *The Nutcracker*. What an amazing experience for her, though, in the end, Barbara's career was short-lived. When we were around ten years of age, Miss O. began to let us take company class at a small, mouse-infested studio on Pape Avenue. Mice or not, we were just happy to be dancing near the people we wanted to be.

When the Company moved to St. Lawrence Hall on King Street, we started doing six-week summer school programmes. As young dancers we could watch the company class take place on the stage in the grand old studio. If it rained, dancers would have to dance around pails strategically placed on the floor to catch the drips from the old ceiling. Watching the classes, we really got to know the dancers, and of course we were able to bother them for their autographs. Those summer schools were a unique time. We would only get two weeks off for summer holidays. Miss O. was still ballet mistress for the Company but was also still running her own school. She kept us under her wing, just as though we were her own children.

Then in 1959, Miss O., with Celia Franca, officially began the National Ballet School, now called Canada's National Ballet School. Miss O. spoke to my parents to invite me to be one of the first students at the School, however, my parents could not afford the eight hundred dollars for tuition. Miss O. set out to find me a scholarship and she found it with the Ladies Auxillary. I was awarded a six-hundred-dollar grant each year for the five years that I was at the School. We started out in a small classroom at 410 Jarvis Street and the Quaker Church on Maitland was the main dance studio. Once the School started, we younger dancers didn't see as much of the Company as we had before.

In 1960, the Company was presenting *Aurora's Wedding.* Our little group—there were six of us and we were all about thirteen—danced a number near the beginning of the ballet. These were our first steps on the Royal Alexandra stage. We had arrived. Maybe just as little bunny fairies, but on the stage nonetheless. From there on, Miss O. took on the role of school principal, full-time. Though Miss O. is something of a polarizing figure for many, she taught me my first *plié* and watched as I danced my first performance. I became a ballerina much in part because of the opportunities and time Miss O gave to me. For this reason, my feelings towards her have always been of love and gratitude. She was like a second mother to me.

I thank her for everything she did. Miss O. was a pioneer of dance in this country. And with the help of Celia Franca they forged the Ballet School and Company we have today. I was lucky to have a love of dance from a young age and that it turned into a long career.

—Vanessa Harwood

ANTONY TUDOR

ANTONY TUDOR HAD BOTH an indirect and a direct influence on the founding and development of the National Ballet of Canada. Born in London in 1908, and considered a titan of twentieth century ballet, he began his training at age nineteen, in 1927, with Marie Rambert of the Ballet Rambert. He choreographed his first ballet for this company, *Cross-Gartered,* in 1931 at age twenty-three, drawing on Shakespeare's *Twelfth Night.* In 1938 he founded his own company, the London Ballet, and in 1939, at age thirty-one, left London for the United States, where he was a dancer and choreographer for the American Ballet Theatre in New York for a decade. He was part of the ballet and ballet

Anthony Tudor. Courtesy: National Ballet Archives

school of the Metropolitan Opera, and taught at the Juilliard School of Music.

Tudor is known primarily for his dramatic psychological productions and choreography, such as the tragic *Dark Elegies* in 1937 and comic *Gala Performance* in 1938. He created *Lilac Garden* in 1936 on the themes of grief, jealousy, rejection, and frustration. He always made clever use of the *corps de ballet.*

Tudor was one of a number of mid-twentieth century choreographers to create a more dramatic and psychological form of ballet (Cranko and Forsythe in Germany, and Bejart and Petit in France also contributed to this form). In doing this, they also drew on and developed the skills of new types of dancers. One of the significant persons influenced by Tudor's work was the New York City Ballet's George Balanchine.

Because Tudor and Franca had worked together at the Ballet Rambert, he gave his ballets to the National Ballet of Canada. This gift was a big boost to the Company in the early years. Lilian Jarvis notes that her "most enjoyable later roles were also in keeping with my lyrical and character preference," such as dancing the part of the Sister in *Lilac Garden*. Yves Cousineau states that working with Tudor moved him forward in his dancing. "The pleasure of getting under the skin of a personage. To advance, but also to play. Thank you Antony Tudor.... Tudor's musicality was remarkable. For years we were able to have his ballet *Dark Elegies* (music by Gustav Mahler), a gem rarely seen today, made for a small stage."

—Jocelyn Terell

LOIS SMITH

LOIS SMITH WAS BORN IN HUMBLE SURROUNDINGS to working-class parents at the end of a trail called Pandora Street in Burnaby, British Columbia. The attending midwife pronounced that newborn Lois would one day be famous because "she was born with a veil covering her"—a poetic euphemism for a remnant of the amniotic sac. Lois's English immigrant father was a shoemaker. He encouraged his daughter's love of sports, especially gymnastics. When she was six, a family friend offered to pay for ballet classes but her proud parents declined. Four years later her older brother Bill contributed enough from his job for Lois to attend a weekly class at the British Columbia School of Ballet. He lost his job six months later and the ballet classes abruptly ended. After grade ten, Smith enrolled in a commercial school. She saved enough from summer jobs to take daily ballet class at the Rosemary Deveson School of Dance and within seven months had acquired enough technical skill to audition for and be accepted into Theatre Under the Stars.

By the summer of 1949, when nineteen-year-old Lois Smith met David Adams, she had already acquired considerable stage experience. She had become a featured artist at Theatre Under the Stars, and been hired for a lengthy North American tour of *Oklahoma* including Smith's first performance in Toronto.

Lois Smith and David Adams in Encore! Encore!, *1986. Photo: Marilyn Westlake.*
Courtesy: Lois Smith Electronic Archive at Dance Collection Danse.

Winnipeg-born Adams, in his mid-teens, had joined Gweneth Lloyd's fledging Winnipeg Ballet. In 1946, he went to London to perform and met Celia Franca. In 1948, he returned to Canada and re-joined the Winnipeg Ballet, where he continued to dance and choreograph. In 1949, he took a contract as leading man with Theatre Under the Stars. Lois and David married within the year and they had a daughter in April 1951.

At this time Celia Franca was well advanced with her plans for a national ballet company. She dearly wanted twenty-two-year-old Canadian dancer David Adams. Lois Smith had an impressive background in musical theatre, but limited experience in classical ballet. Adams issued an ultimatum: hire his wife too, or Franca could not have him. So Franca agreed to hire Lois, sight unseen. She had no cause to regret it. There had been other gifted Canadian female dancers before her and there were others among the ranks of the National Ballet in its formative years, but exceptional talent and the circumstances of her professional environment conspired to propel Lois Smith to become Canada's first home-grown prima ballerina.

Smith—elegant, graceful, and dramatically compelling—won the hearts of audiences as the young National Ballet criss-crossed North America. Meanwhile the CBC's new television service, launched in 1952, created new opportunities for disseminating the arts across the country. Franca, who already had experience adapting ballet for the small screen in London, worked with producer Norman Campbell to broadcast the National Ballet to a mass audience. In the process, the Ballet's leading dancers, particularly Lois Smith, acquired a level of recognition unimaginable to earlier generations. This was amplified by her star partnership with her husband, David Adams. Adams' virility and attentive partnering served to highlight Smith's delicate femininity. Smith's natural poise and authority—often the cool counter to Adams' pyrotechnical heat—soon won her a devoted public following. While he partnered many ballerinas, it was the magical quality he and Smith projected on stage— their physical and emotional compatibility—that made them true celebrities.

—Michael Crabb

David Adams and Lois Smith.
Courtesy: Lois Smith Electronic Archives at Dance Collection Danse.

Lois Smith and David Adams in The Nutcracker, *1951. Photo: Ballard and Jarrett.*
Courtesy: National Ballet Archives.

DAVID ADAMS

DAVID ADAMS' DANCE CAREER BEGAN in 1938, at the age of ten, when he auditioned for and became one of the few male members of the Winnipeg Ballet Club. Within a short time, he would become a charter member of the Winnipeg Ballet Company. David's first stage appearances, only one year later, were part of a Cavalcade of Welcome for King George VI and Queen Elizabeth during their visit to Winnipeg in 1939. In 1945, at the age of seventeen, David went on tour with the company—the first tour of Canada by a Canadian ballet company. It was not long before he began to dance some lead roles, following in the footsteps of previous soloist, Paddy Stone, who departed from the company in 1946.

In April of that year, David received a scholarship to study at the Sadler's Wells School in London, England. On September 26, 1946, David departed from Canada, setting sail for England on *The Aquitania*. He was to stay at least one year, studying the art of dance, with the possibility of accepting performance opportunities. At ages eighteen and nineteen, David worked with many influential choreographers and danced in several productions with both the Sadler's Wells Company and the Metropolitan Ballet. Some highlights were dancing with the Russian ballerina Svetllana Beriosova and with the English dancer, Celia Franca, with whom David would later reconnect during the formation of the National Ballet of Canada.

David returned to Canada in October of 1948, and soon began staging many of the classics for the Winnipeg Ballet Company, sharing the expertise he had gained while he was in England. In 1949, at the age of twenty, David created *Ballet Composite*, his first piece of choreography. This new work received good reviews and became part of the company's repertoire. It caught the eye of Mara McBirney, a British teacher living in Vancouver, who offered David a job to teach at her studio. He accepted and signed a contract to perform with Theatre Under the Stars in the upcoming summer season.

It was during his time in Vancouver, dancing "under the stars," that he met the first love of his life, Lois Smith. They danced together in *Song of Norway*, receiving several standing ovations, with an extended tour in Victoria. David and Lois soon became technically brilliant and popular ballet stars as premier principal dancers with the National Ballet of Canada. Throughout the 1950s, the Company toured across Canada, the U.S., and Mexico City. In May of 1961, David decided to seek new opportunities abroad; he returned to England at the age of thirty-three, without Lois. He joined London's Festival Ballet, eventually dancing with that company full-time in 1964. He danced many lead roles and toured several places in Europe, Israel, and South America.

At the invitation of Kenneth MacMillan, David joined the Royal Ballet in 1971 to partner Lynn Seymour in the ballet *Anastasia*. He also danced several character roles, toured with the company all over the world, taught *pas de deux* classes, and directed a subcompany, Ballet for All. In 1977, at age forty-seven, he returned to Canada to take the position of ballet master with the Alberta Ballet Company.

David Adams' amazing contributions to dance in Canada are best described in the eloquent words of Gunnar Blodgett. This tribute to David's legacy was incorporated into the Citation, read by Adrienne Clarkson, former Governor General of Canada, at his investiture ceremony when David was awarded the Officer of the Order of Canada. The citations reads as follows:

"One of our first stars of ballet, David Adams, has had an enormous influence on Canadian dance. A founding member of the National Ballet of Canada, he helped to shape the fledgling company's style. Technical brilliance and superb artistry became its hallmark and, throughout his tenure as principal dancer, choreographer, and ballet master, he dazzled audiences with magnificent productions. Former technical director, ballet master, teacher and choreographer of the Edmonton Festival Ballet and Grant McEwan College, he has shared his immense talent with generations of performers and his impact will resonate for years to come."

—Meredith Adams

LAWRENCE ADAMS, THE DANCER

ALTHOUGH HE DANCED IN THE SHADOW of his famous brother, David Adams, Lawrence Adams was an excellent dancer and a non-conformist at heart. In 1955, he joined the National Ballet of Canada, dancing mainly in the *corps de ballet*. He also danced the part of Friend in Tudor's *Lilac Garden* as my partner. He left the National Ballet in 1961 to join *Les grands ballets de Montreal*, then in 1962 went to New York's Joffrey Ballet, returning to the National Ballet of Canada in 1963. Here he danced as a soloist and principal dancer, known for his athleticism, vitality, and exuberance. He was chosen by Grant Strate to be a peasant in Strate's *The Fisherman and His Soul,* based on Oscar Wilde's fairy tale. He was also one of the dapper young men in Tudor's *Offenbach in the Underworld.* He had beautiful, expressive feet and a natural dancer's body. Upon his return to the National Ballet, he created two memorable roles: Mercutio in Cranko's *Romeo and Juliet* and later the Captain in Cranko's *Pineapple Poll.* In *Romeo and Juliet,* Lawrence was spectacular, full of mischief, hilarity, and bantering friendship to Earl Kraul's Romeo. I had joined the National Ballet Company for the Carter-Barron engagement in Washington, DC, and was in the audience where I witnessed a truly wonderful evening when Lawrence's performance as Mercutio brought down the house. Much later he danced the Captain in *Pineapple Poll* to rave reviews. Lilian Jarvis, who knew *Pineapple Poll* well, wrote: "I'd never tire of Lawrence's musicality, precision, and immersion as the Captain in *Poll.*"

Miss Franca had hoped that Lawrence would form a partnership with Martine van Hamel, as she had cast them together in the Snow Scene of *Nutcracker* as Prince and Snow Queen, as well as in *La Bayedere* Act II. Unfortunately, Martine went on to the American Ballet Theatre and Lawrence left to found Dance Collection Danse (DCD) and "15" Laboratorium. He had already proven that he was a formidable dancer, but he found the ballet world too restricting.

—Jocelyn Terell

LAWRENCE ADAMS, THE VISIONARY

SUMMER 1973: In "New Homes for Dance in Toronto," an article for *Performing Arts in Canada,* I wrote, "The new group of four dancers called '15' are liberated from many conventional dance hang-ups. Their first work was in a sense the process of making the George Street place, which they have longingly done by themselves. Their forty-one-seat theatre is a little gem, vibrating with promises of future experiments and discoveries."

I described an untitled dance by Miriam. "Lawrence Adams and Diane Drum lie asleep in pyjamas in the centre of the arena. Sometimes Lawrence gets up and does something like the Twist. A bad dream of a ballerina (Miriam Adams) in warm-up attire clumps in. She is swathed in plastic and her dancing is hard as nails. Time passes. She sheds her clothes layer by layer as she fiercely goes about her work. From time to time, Lawrence jumps up to lift her briefly in balletic flight. Lawrence says some hilarious things about dance and art in connection with what goes on "under the sheets." It is a crazy vision of a dance, which one would willingly return to."

Over the next three decades, I returned many times to see Lawrence and Miriam, marvelling at the activity they initiated through the "15" Dance Laboratorium, the *Encore! Encore!* reconstructions and Dance Collection Danse (DCD).

Lawrence's brilliant work and unconventional leadership inspired many to remember him in words. Tributes by colleagues and a succinct biography by Paula Citron are collected in *DCD Magazine Issue 56* (2003). Articles in the anthology, *Renegrade Bodies: Canadian Dance in the 1970s,* edited by Allana C. Lindgren and Kaija Pepper (2012) provide further insights and context. Mentored by Lawrence in his last years, Amy Bowring completed Lawrence's extremely useful *Building Your Legacy: An Archiving Handbook for Dance* (2004) and distributed hundreds of copies to dancers and students.

"Dance power"—dance legacy—yes!

—Selma Odom

ANGELA LEIGH

ANGELA LEIGH WAS ENDURINGLY CREATIVE as a ballerina, artist, and teacher. As a teacher in the dance program at York University, she was a revelation—exotic, stylish, outspoken, and idiosyncratic. Angela had recently studied yoga in India and started each class with yoga practice, highly unorthodox in the early 1970s. She had embraced the free-spiritedness of the late sixties and early seventies, dressed in flowing clothes, and often with a scarf bound around her blonde curls. Angela had a keen sense of humour, and a nonjudgmental approach that coaxed out students' latent aspirations and talents. She shared her passion for motion, imparting lyricism and deep physicality in her ballet classes.

Born in 1927 in Uganda, Angela studied ballet in London with the Royal Ballet, where she worked with John Cranko. After World War II, she and her family immigrated to Canada. She started teaching in Barrie and Orillia but soon gravitated to Toronto. Celia Franca hired Leigh as a principal dancer and charter member of the National Ballet Canada. Angela's friend, Joysanne Sidimus, recalls that she was "very beautiful, long, lean, fine-boned with long, elegant feet" and that Franca recognized her potential to impart a sense of glamorous femininity to the fledgling National Ballet, at that time largely populated by very young dancers. Angela danced most of the lead classical and contemporary roles, including the Black Swan in *Swan Lake* to Jocelyn Terell's White Swan Queen, partnered by Earl Kraul. She was often partnered by Joey Harris, known professionally as Ivan Demidoff. Angela could make difficult choreography work for her, recalls Sidimus, as she was a sophisticated mover. For example, Grant State's *Triptych,* set to the Mozart clarinet concerto was a challenging choreography that she somehow managed to do well and with aplomb.

Angela's second marriage to Canadian filmmaker and writer, Paul Almond, connected her with many luminaries in film and television. In 1963, she landed a lead role in the film, *The Other Man.* She constantly re-invented herself in creative ways. She would go on to teach and coach at Canada's National Ballet School and the National Ballet of Canada. She became an assistant professor of York University and taught at George Brown College. She delved into choreography, creating work with the National Ballet School, Dancemakers, the Canadian Opera Company, and Ontario Ballet Theatre. She was also a talented designer who had a penchant for renovating and decorating houses, and worked on residential and commercial properties. As a fabric artist, she created unique silk garments, paintings, and décor. When she moved to Victoria, she became an advisor to Ballet Victoria, the company she had helped found. Angela Leigh is vividly remembered for the bold and creative *elan* with which she danced through life.

—Carol Anderson

TERESA MANN

MY MOTHER, TERESA MANN, WAS AN ARTIST. If I could describe her in two phrases, I would say she loved to dance, and she loved God. These two descriptions summed up her whole life, her entire self, her reason for existing.

Her mother, Rosaura de Obarrio was Panamanian and her father, Henry Mann, who came to Panama with the Royal Bank of Canada, was Canadian. Teresa was born in Panama but at age two the family moved to Caracas, Venezuela, where she began her dance lessons. A few years later, the family moved again, to Lima, Peru, where they lived for several years and she continued her passion for dance. After high school she moved back to Panama where she became one of the founding students of the National Ballet School of Panama. By that point all she wanted to be was a ballet dancer. Eventually she moved to New York City to pursue her dance career. There she saw the National Ballet of Canada perform for the first time. She fell in love with the Company and enrolled in a National Ballet of Canada summer course in Toronto. Celia Franca offered Theresa a contract to join the dance company.

My mother danced with the National Ballet for five years, from 1956 to 1961. She told stories about their tours and the hours spent on buses. She said there were several buses, one for principals and soloists, another for the *corps* members and one for the orchestra. She made lifelong friends like Shirley Kash (Tetreau), a dancer and later a teacher at the National Ballet School, and Mary McDonald, their pianist. My mother had a deep admiration for her colleagues of those early years: Brian

Earl Kraul and Teresa Mann. Courtesy: Private collection.

Macdonald and David Scott, Joanne Nisbet, David Adams, Lawrence Adams, Lorna Geddes, Victoria Bertram, Mary Jago, Jocelyn Terell, Beverly Banfield, Jeannette Cassels, Collen Kenney, Angela Leigh, Brian Madonald, Ian Robertson, and Grant Strate. She and Earl Kraul, who was principal dancer in the early years, would become friends and she convinced him to come be a guest artist with the National Ballet of Panama. They danced together and had great respect for one another. Some other dancers from those early years in the Company would also end up as my teachers, such as Lilian Jarvis and Glenn Gilmour. My mother was also very good friends with Patricia Neary who became a principal dancer with New York City Ballet and worked with George Balanchine, the famous choreographer. My mother held great admiration for Celia Franca. She spoke to me about her strict discipline and work ethic. I would often hear about her and Betty Oliphant, cofounder of the National Ballet School.

Teresa Mann danced until she was fifty. For her last performance she danced *The Dying Swan* in her Teatro Municipal of Lima, the same theatre where she danced for the first time at the age of five. Once she knew she wanted to retire, she danced five more years, "to be totally sure," she told me. I always admired that strength, determination, and commitment in her. She was a strong woman.

—Myriam Mann

EARL KRAUL

EARL KRAUL WAS A TAPPER BY NINE, but in his teens was inspired to pursue ballet by Eugene Loring's *Billy the Kid*. Two years after joining the National, he was promoted to soloist where he drew critical attention. In July 1951, the Toronto drama critic, Herbert Whittaker picked out "the promising Earl Kraul." In his review of their launch that November, Whittaker described *Études*, the *pas de quatre* featuring Earl, as "the most encouraging, refreshing item on the program, while praising his "vitality and attack" in the *Polovtsian Dances*. Critics around the continent agreed. Accounts of Earl as a dancer on the rise included "dazzling exhibition—inordinately powerful—soaring with grace belying his strength." Versatility, too, was apparent early on. His work in the western-themed *Ballad* was described as "violent and passionate," his performance in Strate's *The Fisherman and His Soul* praised as "dramatic, fantastic, and full of pathos."

Audiences responded to Earl. They felt his momentum and were moved by his emotional depth. He had, as well, the striking good looks of a hero from a Norse myth. Vancouver's Robert Sunter wrote that Earl Kraul's "empathy has made him Canada's premier dancer," his work was "full of grace and fluid, muscular vitality." He was relentless in the face of technical challenges, yet moved with ease and a velvety tread.

We admired him above all, however, for his creativity in roles and for the personality he brought to the stage. From his boyish charm as Franz in *Coppelia* to his anguish as Orestes in Strate's *House of Atreus,* Earl was a dancer who put story first. He was enigmatic and soulful in *Solitude* and brought tragic desperation to *Les Sylphides*. Most of all we were stirred by his conviction as the star-crossed lover in John Cranko's *Romeo and Juliet*. As Romeo, Earl created a signature role for himself and helped establish a new phase in the National Ballet's history. He was the home-grown Canadian who so movingly embodied the famous lover and, with Veronica Tennant, personified the company's coming of age.

In those heady days of the *Romeo and Juliet* launch, we watched, enthralled, as Veronica blossomed in his sensitive hands. But it was more than partnering technique on display. He was first and foremost a lover. From the moment, he spied her in the ballroom scene you felt the lightning sear through his being and later, under the balcony, the waves of their passion flooding the stage.

As a fighter he was equally intense. No one who ever saw them clash could forget his struggles with Yves Cousineau's Tybalt. Yves' Prince of Cats was a formidable foe and their conflict acquired iconic status. In the production's first weeks, an extraordinary event electrified the cast and crystallized awareness that this was a new phase in the Company's identity: Romeo (Kraul) and Tybalt (Cousineau) were locked in their duel when Romeo's rapier snapped off in his hand. He defended

Earl Kraul, Oldyna Dynowska, Katherine Stewart, Natalia Butko, Étude.
Courtesy: Lois Smith Electronic Archives at Dance Collection Danse.

Earl Kraul, Natalia Butko, Katherine Stewart,and Oldyna Dynowska, Étude.
Courtesy: National Ballet Archives.

himself with the hilt and stub of his sword as the music reached its climax, when suddenly Benvolio (Glenn Gilmour) slung his sword toward Romeo, the blade whistling through the air, spinning end over end. On the final, shimmering chord, Romeo grabbed the sword out of the air with his free hand, and dealt Tybalt the final, fatal blow.

Stunts like this had never been seen in the National Ballet before. The ovation lasted longer that night than anyone could remember and the Company was transformed. Those present still marvel at Earl's self-possession in the heat of passion, at his nerve, dexterity, and flair. In that one moment, he brought the artistry and commitment of the entire Company into focus. It was no longer just about dance. We were now in the business of theatre. Nureyev's 1972 *Sleeping Beauty* was arguably made possible by the ongoing *Romeo and Juliet* effect, and especially by Earl's contributions at the heart of the action.

—Timothy Spain,

EARL KRAUL—MY FIRST ROMEO

HOW BLESSED WE WERE TO HAVE the pre-eminent Earl Kraul teach us *pas de deux* in those early (and for me final) years at the National Ballet School. We'd watched his dynamic dancing and his superb partnering with Lois, Lilian, Jocelyn—indeed most of the women dancing with the Company—with awe. He had the gift of charisma, a magnetic stage presence, and was a *premier danseur* of technical accomplishment, dramatic finesse, and irrepressible generosity. Earl, a consummate partner, was an incomparably gifted teacher and I adored those classes where he would coach us novices to understand how the synchronization of our musicality, breaths and *pliés*, our take-offs and mutually protected landings could give reality, and thus illusion, to the choreography. He inspired the men—Sam Moses, David Earle, Andrew Oxenham, John Klampter, and Tim Spain, among others—by unmatchable example and clarity of explanation. And happy were the times when he would demonstrate with me!

Lucky, *lucky* me to be chosen to dance *Les Sylphides* with Earl, Mr. Blue Eyes, in my graduation year. I had a huge crush

Veronica Tennant and Earl Kraul after a performance of Romeo and Juliet, *1964. Courtesy: Private collection.*

on him already! He was strong. He was funny. He was *fun*. I mooned for months over the romance, poetry, and bliss of that experience. And then—after missing a year due to a back injury—I entered the Company in 1964 at eighteen and was cast by the very brave Miss Franca to dance Juliet. While Miss

Franca took an enormous chance on me, she knew what she was doing when she put me in Earl's arms—and he swept me off my feet. If Juliet set the course of my dramatic dancing career, Earl Kraul nurtured the takeoff. Without him I could have neither braved the tightrope path, nor succeeded. For what is Juliet without her Romeo?

So many touching memories flood back from the first performance and every single one after. From that first sight of each other at the ball, those mesmerizing blue eyes made my heart stop. The dreamy madrigals, first touch of palm to palm, the sheer romance of the balcony scene, our first kiss, the bliss of the wedding, the pain of our parting, and the grief of our tragic ending.

I remember Windsor, Ontario, where we toured regularly. Earl took me aside before a performance. With an uncharacteristic seriousness on his face, he said, "I want to have a word with you," and then presented me with an exquisite Georgian garnet pendant for my nineteenth birthday. As a friend, Earl defined generosity and tenderness. And it was my honour to dance with him.

—Veronica Tennant

GRANT STRATE: HIS EARLY LIFE

IN 1950-51, CELIA FRANCA EMBARKED on a nationwide tour to audition dancers for the founding of the National Ballet of Canada. In Edmonton, she first encountered Grant Strate, then a young, untried, primarily modern dancer. With her uncanny ability to intuitively sense potential, she learned he was a graduate lawyer who, after a year of practicing law, decided he'd rather be a dancer. Her instinct led her to someone who evolved over the years from dancer to choreographer-in-residence, and an overall critical voice in the development of the Company's repertoire and policies. During his time with the National Ballet, Strate created twenty works, many involving Canadian composers and designers. A complex and talented man, Strate's challenging, inquiring mind always served as a catalyst for action. While Franca stayed with the Company, she encouraged him to travel,

Grante Strate and Lilian Jarvis in Afternoon of a Faun, *early 1950s. Photo: Ken Bell.*
Courtesy: National Ballet Archives.

seeking both influences and choreographers advantageous to the young company. His most important achievement was bringing John Cranko's *Romeo and Juliet* to the Company, which coincided with a move from the Royal Alexandra Theatre to the then-new four-thousand-seat O'Keefe Centre (now the Sony Centre). It was a tremendous shift for the Company and one that catapulted them into international recognition.

Strate's choreographic process was always interesting, if somewhat improvisatory, perhaps due to his lack of formal balletic training. Though he was rigorously immersed in ballet training once he joined the Company, modern-based movement seemed of great interest to him as a choreographer. At the time, he was planning to choreograph *House of Atreus,* one of three ballets on the Electra theme. The first, a chamber work, had met with great success the previous year when he was a guest at Julliard in New York. This time he was planning a much bigger work—an all-Canadian production with a commissioned score by celebrated composer, Harry Somers, and set and costume design by the famous artist, Harold Town. He had to pull the show together on a short timeline, but it worked. Similarly, when he choreographed *Pulcinella* to a Stravinsky score, there were so many *bourrees* on pointe that all three dancers sharing the role of Pimpinella had to change shoes halfway through the ballet to accommodate this request.

Strate had an action-oriented sense of justice. When he choreographed *Electra* with an electronic score by Henri Pousseur in Glenn Gould's Stratford Summer Music series, he invited Arthur Mitchell, Balanchine's brilliant black principal dancer to portray Orestes to my Electra. This came at the height of the Civil Rights Movement, when television stations in the Southern states refused to show *Agon,* where Arthur did a *pas de deux* with Diana Adams, a white principal dancer. Arthur and I were thrilled to be working together again and both the festival and the Canadian audiences didn't blink an eye.

When visiting artists came to Toronto, his home was the place to go for gatherings. Lynn Seymour, Erik Bruhn, John Cranko, Marcia Haydee, Ray Barra, and many others were welcomed. With his enquiring lawyer's mind, he would probe these great artists to speak of their ideas and creative processes. He was truly a national treasure: unique, iconoclastic, and yet coupled with profound humanity and generosity of spirit rare in the world.

—Joysanne Sidimus

GRANT STRATE: HIS LATER LIFE

GRANT STRATE ALWAYS TOOK a panoramic view of the dance world. So, when he stepped down from the artistic staff of the National Ballet of Canada in 1971 and immediately stepped up to the role of founding director for York University's dance department, it was a means to see farther, in more directions, and with greater objectivity. His mandate at York was to *educate* rather than just train dancers and creators. He built a superlative faculty of artists working within widely varying practices and hosted greats of the dance world as special guest teachers. He sent his students downtown to see Toronto's professional dancers on stage and those dancers came to York to see performances by the companies of Merce Cunningham, Paul Taylor, Mel Wong, and other choreographers from New Your City. Strate wanted to fuel ambitious creativity. As the first graduates left York, dance activity in Toronto suddenly expanded in a multitude of radical new directions: artist-run spaces; durational events; work driven by concept, text and technology; work informed by the politics of race, feminism, sexual orientation and the left.

I remember very clearly the meetings held in his living room for the group of fledgling dancers who would become Dancemakers. He assured us that the work itself would teach us how to become professional, to become the dancers we aspired to be. And I will never forget a rehearsal he directed for Dancemakers in 1974, when we were working on a wonderful piece by Norman Morrice, then Artistic Director of England's Ballet Rambert, and a guest teacher at York. The dance featured Carol Anderson and David Langer. At the end of the rehearsal he shared an abundance of pertinent insights, especially regarding crucial elements of choreography for Carol and David. As he concluded these notes, he paused for a moment, not quite knowing how to work his next thought. Then, he looked at me and said, "And you Peggy, we're going for an Academy Award." His candour could always be counted on.

Grant was a keenly intelligent, openhearted man. He was often described as a "statesman of dance." His life partners, Earl Kraul and later, Wen Wai Wang, were each magnificent companions during his personal and artistic journeys. Grant Strate was a towering presence in Canadian dance. His efforts, influence, and contributions were profound and crucial, and his legacy will continue to move our art form forward for generations to come.

—Peggy Baker

BRIAN MACDONALD

GROWING UP, BRIAN PLAYED THE PIANO and was a child actor for CBC radio, standing on a phonebook to reach the microphone. He was a student at McGill University when he first saw a rehearsal of George Balanchine's *Concerto Barocco* with the New York City Ballet. The Company was in Montreal and they had asked if McGill knew of a studio where they could rehearse. Brian was dispatched to tell them yes, and while watching the rehearsal, he knew his life was changed forever. In that moment he decided that ballet and choreography would be what he was going to do. His first teacher, Gerald Crevier, told Brian, "Start with the little children and learn everything from the beginning." He also trained with Elisabeth Leese.

After graduating from McGill, Brian auditioned for Celia Franca, and was accepted into the Company that became the National Ballet of Canada. The pay was meagre and sometimes Brian would wash the studio floor to earn extra. To make ends meet, there were four or five male dancers sharing an apartment. Among them was Grant Strate. The men would share the cooking—"There was lots of Jell-o." It was supposed to be good for the joints and it was cheap. Towards the end of the week the funds would run out and the women in the Company would invite the "guys" home for a proper Sunday dinner that their mothers would cook.

Oldyna Dynowska and Brian Macdonald in Ballet Behind Us, *1951.*
Photo: Ballard and Jarrett. Courtesy: National Ballet Archives.

Brian loved Celia's classes as she was a dancer herself and her classes were filled with movement. When Celia organized a choreographic competition within the Company, Brian won the first prize of sixty dollars and was able to buy himself a winter coat. When Olivia Wyatt joined the Company, they became a couple, and during off-season would go the Montreal, where Brian would choreograph for nightclubs or write reviews for the *Montreal Herald.* At one point, he broke his arm, which meant he could no longer partner, so he turned to a long career as a choreographer and director. The two of them directed and choreographed a wildly successful production called *My Fur Lady*, a satirical musical, which toured Canada with over four hundred performances. Subsequently, Olivia joined the Royal Winnipeg Ballet as a dancer, while Brian was named the Company's resident choreographer. After the untimely death of Olivia, Brian went to the Banff School of Fine Arts, to New York, Europe, and Russia on Canada Council grants. He was setting one of his ballets with the Royal Swedish Ballet where he met and married Annette Wiedersheim-Paul, later changed to Annette av Paul. During his career, Brian became Artistic Director of the Royal Swedish Ballet, the Batsheva Ballet in Israel, the Harkness Ballet of New York, *Les Grands Ballets Canadiens* in Montreal and the Summer Dance Program at the Banff Centre. He was also Associate Director of the Stratford Festival and the National Arts Centre in Ottawa.

Among Brian's many choreographic works, *Rose Latulipe,* commissioned for the 1967 Centennial Anniversary of Canada, stands out. It was filmed by the CBC. Add to this, *Star Crossed,* Brian's version of *Romeo and Juliet; Firebird;* as well as *Time Out of Mind; Tam Ti Delam; The Shining People of Leonard Cohen; Double Quartet;* and *Adieu Robert Schumann.*

In 1967, Brian was a recipient of the Order of Canada, elevated to a Companion of the Order of Canada. As well, he received the Molson Prize, Walter Carsen Prize, and the Governor General's Award for Excellence in the Performing Arts. In 2012, the City of Stratford Festival Theatre honoured Brian with a Bronze Star in front of the Avon Theatre.

I was fortunate to inspire, create, and dance many of his ballets and share fifty years of artistic companionship and love with him.

—Annette av Paul

GLENN GILMOUR

GLENN GILMOUR WAS AN INSPIRING DANCER and teacher for generations of dancers in Canada. I had the cherished privilege of working closely with him for over thirty years, first as one of his students at Canada's National Ballet School, later as his teaching colleague at the same institution, and finally as his boss—although the official label "boss" always felt like a misnomer as I never stopped learning from Glenn.

In 1970, all the National Ballet School students, myself among them, were deeply saddened by the news of Glenn's retirement from the National Ballet of Canada. We were devoted fans who deeply regretted that we would no long be able to see him dance his many roles of note, most especially his much-admired performances of Benvolio, but our sadness at no longer seeing him onstage was tempered by the exciting news that he was coming to the School to study teaching with Margaret Saul and Betty Oliphant. We were agog that he would be at the School every day. When he arrived, every glimpse of Glenn resulted in our daring one another to strike up a conversation that inevitably ended in a request for an autograph. These requests became so frequent that Betty eventually had to rescue Glenn by putting a freeze on these autograph appeals.

Within a year of coming to the National Ballet School, Betty hired Glenn as a full-time teacher and I was fortunate to be in his first group of students. Glenn did not disappoint. He brought all the passion for dance he had displayed on stage to his teaching in the classroom. As his students, we always felt closely connected to all the reasons we had fallen in love with ballet in the first place. His carefully crafted *enchainements* and his musical sensitivity turned every exercise into a joyful exploration of the art form and furthered our development as artists. Students were so appreciative of his training that many alumni returned regularly during their holidays to rejoin his classes. But it was not only dancers who recognized his extraordinary musicality. For the next three decades, the School's musicians jockeyed for the chance to be partnered with him in creative classroom collaboration.

Glenn's mastery of the language of dance was evident in everything he choreographed. His exam classes were works of art, his lecture demonstrations a pure joy to interpret, and the pieces he created for School's annual Spring Performances were inspiring for both the dancers and the audience. Perhaps the best known of his ballets was *Playing Field*, based on William Loring's *Lord of the Flies,* which he brought to life in concert with two of his favourite musical partners, Trevor McLain and Robert Swerdlow. Performed four times over fifteen years, *Playing Fields* proved a seminal experience for each of the all-male casts.

Generous as a teacher, Glenn was equally generous as a teaching colleague. He was someone I was able to turn to in moments of self-doubt. He had a straightforward, no-nonsense view of life. This approach, combined with his sense of humour would have me back on track with a spring in my step and hope in my heart, which is why, when Betty Oliphant offered me the opportunity to succeed her as the National Ballet School's Artistic Director, Glenn was the first person I turned to for advice. His encouragement to "seize the opportunity," with his promise to support me every step of the way, meant the world to me. The ways in which Glenn delivered on his promise were an ongoing source of strength for almost twenty years, until his death in 2007.

When Glenn shared his cancer diagnosis with me eighteen months prior to his passing, we agreed on two points. Firstly, that the news of his diagnosis would remain confidential. And secondly, that he would continue teaching for as long as possible. This he did until just two weeks prior to his death. Somehow, even as his physical strength diminished, his love of teaching and his students made him an even more powerful force.

After Glenn's death, there was a groundswell of momentum to pay tribute to his inspiring contributions to so many, and absolute consensus that the celebration of Glenn's life had to take place in National Ballet School's Betty Oliphant Theatre. Although I think Glenn would have been astonished by the need to conduct the tribute twice in a row in order to accommodate everyone wishing to attend, none of us was surprised. On that day, the outpouring of love for Glenn and heartfelt expressions of gratitude for everything he had done through his lifetime were irrefutable evidence of a life more than well-lived.

Thank you, Glenn, from all of us lucky enough to have known you.

—Mavis Staines

DAVID SCOTT AND JOANNE NISBET

HOW WELL I REMEMBER David Scott and Joanne Nisbet's dedication. The pair moved to Canada from England in 1958, invited by Celia Franca to join her then-fledgling National Ballet of Canada as dancers. They soon found—or Celia Franca soon discovered in them—their mutual calling to head up her

David Scott and Joanne Nisbet. Courtesy: Private collection

ballet staff. Conducting rehearsals, teaching class, delivering post-performance corrections—all of these roles essential to the everyday operations of a ballet company were given the age-old hierarchical titles of Ballet Master and Ballet Mistress and David and Joanne wore these titles well. Joanne transitioned earlier from dancing and took on her position first. Later she would relish the pleasure she felt when reading a press caption that said, *David Scott, Ballet Master and his Mistress, Joanne Nisbet.*

David and Joanne were unstinting in their commitment, indefatigable in carrying out Miss Franca's vision—they were her officers of excellence. Gentle, compassionate Joanne gave daily classes, much more than just warm-ups, whether in the studio or onstage just before performances. She was always mindful of our injuries and fatigue, our "glass ankles" as she so aptly called them. David was possessed with the devil of detail. He missed nothing and was a craftsman who unrelentingly emphasized the fundamental refining-points of ballet technique in performance. Both David and Joanne coached and rehearsed and taught the Company dancers every step for Celia's chosen ballets. They served all the visiting choreographers—Antony Tudor, John Cranko, Erik Bruhn—with unreserved commitment and respect.

David once told me that while he didn't always agree with Celia's casting choices, he spoke emphatically about his belief in her standards of excellence for the National Ballet as a major company. Together he and Joanne developed a mandate for the implementation of professionalism, uniformity of style, and a signature vocabulary articulating a specialized movement language. Ballet dancers, especially the *corps*, have a certain "look" which is essential to develop in order to define a company of the first rank. For example, a ballet company is defined and judged by its ability to create single arcs of sweeping movement across the two dozen bodies that populate the *corps,* as can be found in famous ballets such as *Swan Lake, La Bayadère* and *Les Sylphides.* In forging a professional ballet company in those early days, David and Joanne shared one mind with Celia's insistence on reinforcing group endeavour, a support system of coaching,

Irene Apiné and Jury Gotshalks in Coppelia, 1953. Photo: Ken Bell.
Courtesy: National Ballet Archives.

Irene Apiné and Jury Gotshalks in The Nutcracker, 1952. *Photo: John Grange.*
Courtesy: National Ballet Archives.

applied motivation, and a pooled knowledge that worked in tandem with the love of the art.

David Scott recently passed at the age of ninety. For four decades, the National Ballet of Canada was his life and we are deeply indebted to him and to our dear Joanne, who survives him. I can still hear their voices so clearly, though sadly, they are slowly beginning to fade.

—Veronica Tennant

IRENE APINÉ AND JURY GOTSHALKS

IN 1952, JURY AND IRENE WERE DANCING the *Don Quixote pas de deux* for the first time in rehearsal in St. Lawrence Hall on King Street West in Toronto. The two were preparing for the first performances of then newly formed company, the National Ballet of Canada. They danced explosively with acrobatic choreography, multiple turns, and daring lifts. This was new and exciting, a style we had not yet seen within the Company.

Celia Franca had invited the pair to join the group from Halifax where they had lived on arriving in Canada from Riga, Latvia. Jury was instantly cast as the Tartar Warrior Chief in the Polovtsian dances from the Russian opera, *Prince Igor,* an important ballet on the company's opening night. Jury was charismatic, handsome, and an excellent partner, especially for his wife, Irene Apiné. We were shaken by their work, their demanding personalities, their aloofness. They were *bravura* dancers and one felt both cursed and blessed by their pyrotechnic style. I felt a sense that they wanted to assimilate but just could not take that leap; we were so young and inexperienced compared to them. They were too European. After all, they had been leading dancers in the Latvian National Ballet. They had been forced out for political reasons and were unable to dance, either at all, or at their technical, professional level. The National Ballet of Canada was an opportunity for them to recreate and reinvent themselves as thrilling leading dancers of this new Canadian company. Irene was a high-energy, daredevil ballerina. She was beautiful and in all her roles sought the extra high arabesque, or the longer held balance. I loved their Slavic insolence. They were a great addition to the early days of the National Ballet of Canada, but as the repertoire changed, their *bravura* style was no longer appropriate and subtler ballets like *Offenbach in the Underworld* took over.

—Judie Colpman

MARY MCDONALD

MARY MCDONALD WAS A MUCH BELOVED accompanist of thirty-five years with the National Ballet of Canada. Peter Ottmann was only ten years old when he first performed in a production of *The Nutcracker*. He remembers Mary McDonald as a cheerful, motherly figure who made the children feel less lonely, fed them candies, and pinched their cheeks with her strong pianist fingers!

Mary was a wonderful musician and would often play four-handed piano with Celia Franca, who was highly musical herself. As principal pianist, she helped nurture the talent of many young dancers and won the hearts of every visiting artistic director or guest artist including the likes of Sir Frederick Ashton, Anthony Dowell, Rudolf Nureyev, Eric Bruhn, and many, many more. She toured extensively with the Company, accompanying some of the world's most renowned performers, from Karen Kain to Rudolph Nureyev and Mikhail Baryshnikov. While on a trip to Russia in 1973, accompanying Kain and Frank Augustyn at the Moscow International Ballet Competition, Mary was given the top award as pianist, ahead of pianists from twenty-two other countries.

Mary followed pianist Reg Godden in playing Rachmaninoff's highly challenging second piano concerto for the ballet, *Winter Night*. She was endlessly patient when providing accompaniment during rehearsals, given the countless repetitions required. She had a close attachment to dancers taking the floor and saw it as her duty to merge her music with their movements as seamlessly as she could. Mary had high standards and strong opinions about striving for excellence. If an artist, a dancer, a musician, or conductor was not giving their best, she had something to say about it. These were the only moments she wavered from her gregarious and bubbly spirit.

Mary was above all a great believer in and encourager of dancers. Her attitude provided a rare reprieve in a culture that thrives on punitive pedagogies. Mary was amazingly modest, never assuming that she deserved any credit for the Company's successes, though she did indeed. She was a kind, generous, and loving person. She will always be greatly missed by all of those her music and spirit touched.

—Jocelyn Terell and Peter Ottmann

GEORGE CRUM

THE ONE THING ANYONE WHO KNEW George Crum would remember about him was his love of telling jokes. Give him five seconds of your time and he would be asking you, "Did I tell you the one about…?" His face would already be crinkling up in anticipation of sharing your laughter. Never missing a beat once started, he would often break up, tears welling in his eyes, scarcely getting to the end of the story.

Beyond his humour, George Crum was multi-talented, his position as first conductor of the National Ballet only one of his many virtues. Absorbing his love of opera was something I did really appreciate. Along with his wife, Pat, and my husband at the time, Dick Butterfield, I enjoyed many an evening listening to Verdi and Puccini operas while George pointed out musical nuances that made the soaring music all the more moving. George's introduction to this magnificent art form added a dimension to my life that I am ever grateful for, and value to this day.

George's talents found other outlets as well. He was a superb craftsman in woodworking and took pleasure in designing beautiful bowls and boxes, a sampling of which I'm fortunate to have in my possession. His creative spirit was infectious and he would sit for me during tour stops while I drew portraits of him. Aside from his various artistic endeavours and his excellence as a conductor, George was also an avid golfer and billiards enthusiast—his interests ran the gamut.

George never tired—at least it seemed that way—of the endless repetitions of *The Nutcracker, Les Sylphides, Gala Performance* and other ballets that comprised our small repertoire in the early days. With his eyes always on the dancers to follow our lead, he seldom gave us the wrong tempo and, if he did, would be quick to change it for the next time around. With his patience and sincere interest in helping us do our best, George was the perfect dancers' conductor.

I am sure that many dancers from those early days have their own personal memories of George, but one that I'm sure all of us remember is the time a piano he was helping to move fell on his foot and broke it. Undaunted, he cheerfully conducted through the following weeks with a cast on his foot; neither the dancers nor the audience were negatively affected. George always gave his best and lived up to the unspoken motto, as did the rest of us, that "the show must go on, regardless." Jocelyn Terell adds: "One of George's favourite jokes was about the conductor asking the ballerina each night if she wanted the music too slow or too fast. He told me that one often!"

—Lilian Jarvis

NORMAN CAMPBELL

NORMAN CAMPBELL WAS A DISTINGUISHED television producer who was much beloved by National Ballet dancers. He was a director whose credits ranged from episodes of *All in the Family* and the *Mary Tyler Moore Show* to musical variety specials and opera. However, it was as a director and producer of televised ballet for the Canadian Broadcasting Company that he made a special mark and contributed enormously to the early success of the National Ballet of Canada. Over the years he produced and directed sixteen full-length ballets by the National Ballet of Canada, as well as *The Looking Glass People,* a program about the Company, and numerous variety shows and specials that featured members of the Company. His work won two Emmys, one in 1968 for *Cinderella,* and one in 1972 for *The Sleeping Beauty,* as well as the prestigious Prix Rene Barthelemy in 1966 for *Romeo and Juliet,* all danced by Veronica Tennant.

At university, Campbell majored in math and physics to become a meteorologist. He also became involved in university theatricals. He only studied music for a few years, but he was a natural musician and composer. While working on Sable Island in Nova Scotia, he composed songs and photographed the wild horses, selling these photos to *Saturday Night* and *The Saturday Evening Post*. His appreciation of dramatic narrative, natural musicality, and a photographer's eye, eventually brought him to the adaptation of classical ballet for the television screen. The CBC producer and director, Eric Till, described another gift that Campbell had, "the common touch ... that extraordinary instinct of reaching an audience."

In 1956, CBC supervising producer Robert Allen sought the advice of fellow CBC producer Eric Till on the future programming of ballet. Till advised him, "Since you get criticized for not doing it, why don't you go after the biggest audience you can get and put on the greatest warhorse of all ballets which never fails to attract a huge audience—do *Swan Lake!*" Till was charged with calling Celia Franca, the founder and artistic director of the National Ballet of Canada, to determine if she could do a ninety-minute *Swan Lake*. According to Till her response was, "Of course I can!" Norman Campbell was given the job of producing his first *Swan Lake*.

Celia Franca was interested in television for two reasons. "My concerns with Canadian television were—in addition to the artistic ones—with securing extra employment for our dancers and with reaching a larger audience than the ballet could command in theatres" (Bell 136). Franca was astute enough to recognize that television could give the Company exposure that would be impossible to duplicate through performing and touring.

The resulting 1956 production of *Swan Lake* was broadcast live and its importance for the National Ballet cannot be underestimated. The actor, Barry Morse, introduced the programme and prior to each act gave a brief synopsis of the narrative. Before the fourth and final act, he also commented on the history of the National Ballet then added: "Tonight represents another milestone in the history of *Swan Lake*. This is the very first time that all four acts of the ballet have been presented on North American television and it should be a matter of pride for all Canadians that our National Ballet Company is one of the very few ballet companies in the world to have the full-length version in its repertoire" (Campbell).

The broadcast not only reinforced the Company's prestige, but also its claim to being a national company. Campbell would go on to produce and direct the Company's television productions of *Coppelia, The Nutcracker, Pineapple Poll,* a second version of Franca's *Swan Lake, Giselle* with Lois Smith, *Romeo and Juliet,* Erick Bruhn's *Swan Lake, The Sleeping Beauty, Giselle* with Karen Kain, *La fille mal gardée, Onegin, The Merry Widow, La Ronde* and *Alice.*

Celia Franca summed up Campbell's contribution to the National Ballet well when she said, "Mr. Campbell has contributed more towards exposing the National Ballet to the Canadian public than any of us. He is an artist of ability, taste, imagination, discrimination, honesty, and humour. He has the respect and affection of all who work with him—cameramen, technicians, make-up artists, designers, musicians, dancers and choreographers. His unfailing instinct enables him to bring out exactly the right dynamics in a dramatic or humorous situation and while he believes (as indeed I do) that when ballet is transferred to the screen, the vocabulary of the television medium should be used to the full, he always has respect for the choreography and never distorts the dance form for the sake of gimmickry" (Franca 7).

—Cheryl Belkin Epstein

8.
Life After the National Ballet

TODAY THE NATIONAL BALLET IS THRIVING and so is the National Ballet School. Young students of the School receive ten years of excellent daily ballet training as well as an outstanding Toronto District School Board-approved academic education from grades six to twelve. The curriculum includes courses such as History of Dance, Contemporary Repertoire, Technique, Improvisation, Classical Indian Dance, Anatomy, *Pas de Deux* (Partnering), class with Artist-in-Residence Peggy Baker, and conditioning and cardio from Irene Down, a neuromuscular consultant. These students dance in the morning and study in the afternoon. They are very busy!

In addition, the students have the privilege of learning from internationally renowned guest teachers. In their senior year, students can also choose to go on an exchange trip with any of twenty-four international partner schools. The program is supported by the Federal government, the Ontario provincial government, the City of Toronto, and the Ontario Arts Council.

Perhaps the biggest change the Company has seen in recent years is a shift in its approach to dancers who marry or become parents during their careers. In Franca's day, marriage was seen to be the end of a career in ballet. Even having a boyfriend raised Franca's eyebrows and pricked her fear of losing a dancer to pregnancy. Franca once turned to a musician I was dating and said "Don't get her pregnant," though I had barely been kissed!

Giving birth to a child was considered totally unthinkable, the antithesis to a career. Today, however, marriage and motherhood are accepted and even encouraged. Many couples make up the

National Ballet of Canada and some of them even have a child or two. Of course, an enormous amount of discipline is required to raise a child in the Company.

The early dancers of the fifties have gone on to do many other things after a career dancing with the National Ballet of Canada. Clearly the discipline of dance may be readily applied to other areas.

After a few years with the Company, Edelayne Brandt parted ways due to the newly-found religious beliefs of her parents, which strictly forbade dance. She went on to learn typing and terminology to become a medical secretary in Edmonton. She then married Barry Westgate, an entertainment critic and city columnist at the *Edmonton Journal*. Edelayne spent seventeen years as a copywriter, then became Creative Director of the CYCA and K97 radio stations. She also spent five years auditioning students as the Canadian representative for the University of the Arts, London, England. In 2002, Barry died and Edelayne then began living with her sister, Val, a talented librettist. Together they indulged a lifelong love of travel and passion for the arts—dance, theatre, opera, art exhibits, and concerts around the world. Only occasionally she wonders what might have happened if she had remained with the National Ballet of Canada.

Many of the women married and had children before going on to develop a new career. Judie Colpman married George Brown and together they moved to North Africa—first to Tunisia, then to Morocco. Judie and George had two children—one of whom became a ballet dancer with the New York City Ballet, Pretty Ugly Dance Company, and the Frankfurt Ballet for eleven years. Judie worked as an actor, artistic director, and choreographer—first in Ottawa and then in New York. She writes that, "my experience in the National Ballet of Canada has informed everything I have done since, as an actor, director, choreographer, and teacher." Judie has continued to work in theatre and has had an impressive career in cabaret.

Cathy Carr was injured out of dance. Though not an unusual experience, it is always a moment to mourn. After breaking her metatarsal, she and Celia Franca agreed that Cathy had probably reached her dancing ceiling. She left on good terms, married, and had two daughters. Cathy acquired her BA in Psychology and English, and has worked ever since in the corporate world, always in the health field.

Marcel Chojnacki became a teacher of physical education where he integrated dance into the school curriculum. Though his career in ballet ended, his lifetime dancing did not. Marcel went on to specialize in flamenco dance where he taught, choreographed, and performed. He performed flamenco up to the age of eighty-three. In 1995, at the age of sixty-five, Marcel started taking violin lessons. He then joined Canadian Amateur Musicians/*Musiciens amateurs du Canada* (CAMMAC) in the second violin section, and joined *L'orchestre philarmonie* in the first violin section. Add to this that Marcel also completed a Bachelors of Science by taking night courses over eighteen years—the sorts of accomplishments a dancerly discipline garners are plain to see.

Myrna Aaron was an original member of the National Ballet of Canada, and had the distinction of being the youngest member of the original company. Of her post-ballet life she says, "I now have a doctorate in Psychology … I just did things in a different order."

Sally Brayley became Director of Dance in St. Louis for eleven years, and then became an Executive Director Emeritus, developing education and outreach projects. She was married to Antony Bliss, former manager of the National Metropolitan Opera, with whom she had two sons and two granddaughters. She now lives in St. Louis, Missouri, with her second husband, Jim Connett, manager of the Radio Arts Foundation and of the new classical music station in St. Louis. She has six stepchildren, seven step-grandchildren, and four great grandchildren. Sally has also been on the board of the Joffrey Ballet. After being awarded an honourary member of the organization, she was awarded the *Corps de ballet* International Lifetime Achievement Award in Florence in November 11, 1998. St. Louis also presented Sally with their inaugural presentation of the Annelise Mertz Visionary Award in Dance.

Yves Cousineau travelled to Europe to deepen his training in mime and theatrical arts before returning to dance at the National Ballet. In 1970, he exchanged a life of dance for a life of academics when he joined the Faculty of Dance at York University, eventually becoming the department chair.

After her career with the Ballet ended, Oldyna Dynowska wrote a children's book, then completed a Bachelor's degree at the Brooklyn Centre for the Arts with a major in Art and a minor in Music. She graduated *summa cum laude* and became assistant professor of Dance at the School of Performing Arts in Brooklyn, New York. She later did a Masters of Fine Art in Studio Art.

Pauline McCullagh went on to earn a teaching diploma from Chelsea College of Arts in London, England. She also took courses at the Laban Art of Movement, performed with the Laban dancers, and taught English and Physical Education. She took summer school in Connecticut and California while teaching synchronized swimming. Pauline became a National Synchronized Swimming Champion.

Cecily Paige married and taught the Cecchetti syllabus for thirty-two years in Australia.

Valerie Lyon did a four-year novitiate at the Monastery of the Little Flower of Jesus in Buffalo. She found that many of the skills she cultivated in ballet, such as obedience and joy, transferred well to the monastery. She later was appointed Prioress of the monastery.

Janet Green attended York University, obtaining a Bachelor of Arts in 1969 and a doctorate in 1976. Janet is an author and filmmaker best-known for her CBC television series, *Wild Country Canada*. Based on forty years of photography, filmmaking, and broadcasting, she has shown television audiences Canada's splendid wilderness regions. In 1972, she began working with her husband, John, as a television host and producer, writing in the field of natural sciences programming, making documentaries for the Discovery Channel in Canada. They have received several awards for their work, including Gemini for Best Photography, a Golden Sheep for Best Science and Nature Documentary, and a Directors Award from Friends of Algonquin. Janet has written *A Cabin Full of Noise* (1980), *The Wilds of Whippoorwill Farm* (1982), and *Journey to the Top of the World* (1987). She is co-author of books based on her CBC television series. Janet works with elementary school children across Canada, sharing her passion for wildlife and wilderness places. She and her husband live in a log home on an old farm at the edge of the woods in Eastern, Ontario.

Penny Anne Winter followed a dance career in the National Ballet of Canada and the Festival Ballet with a career as a massage therapist, and finally, after much studying, as a psychotherapist.

Katrina Evanova taught extracurricular dance at Catholic and Metropolitan Separate schools. She married and has two children. After her career with the National Ballet, she performed in commercials, films, and television. In 1982, Katrina's husband passed away. She taught dance until her retirement in 2013, and wrote a novel, *Stage Lights*. She has also written a libretto on the life of the Canadian poet, Pauline Johnson.

After his career in ballet, Donald Mahler worked for the Tudor Trust and also as a choreographer. In 1961, he joined the National Opera under Dame Alicia Markova. In 1967, he assisted Tudor in staging *Echoing and Trumpets*. In 1979 he became Ballet Master for the National Opera. In 1996 he was cast in the principal role of the first American performance of *Echoing and Trumpets*. Later that year he became Ballet Master for the Zurich Ballet.

Gloria Bonnell turned her hand to singing and dancing in TV shows on CBC and at the Canadian Grandstand Show. She embarked on a new career as a mother in the 1960s, and sold real estate briefly in the 1970s. In the 1980s, with the explosion of the "jazzercise" trend, Gloria passed the course to become a jazzercise instructor, surpassing many younger women at her final audition.

Lorna Geddes is *still* with the National Ballet! She has been assistant ballet mistress since 1984 and has taken care of the footwear needs of the Company's dancers since 1998. She still performs as a principal character artist.

Frances Greenwood is now retired after eighteen years as a stockbroker and before that, a long career as a theatrical/TV agent and artist manager in both Toronto and Los Angeles.

Since leaving the National Ballet, Bob Ito has had a long career in film and television, first moving to New York to dance on Broadway in the musical *Flower Drum Song*, then commencing a long career in Los Angeles, best-known for his role as Sam Fujiyama on the show *Quincy, M.E.*

Lilian Jarvis took a year to study Martha Graham technique in New York. That year set her on a new career path away from the National Ballet, developing her own physical and mental alignment program known as Somatic Stretch: The Jarvis Technique. She still teaches this technique at her studio in downtown Toronto and online. She did have one more moment in the spotlight with the National Ballet when she was asked to dance Juliet in the company's twenty-fifth anniversary production of *Romeo and Juliet*.

Shirley Kash initially left the National Ballet Company to become part of the original faculty at the National Ballet School. After several years there as a Cecchetti examiner, she taught and examined at multiple dance schools across Ontario, following her calling to shape new, young dancers.

These dancers' stories are living proof that dance has numerous transferable skills. I am very proud of what they have been able to achieve both in dance and beyond, as I am sure they are as well.

9.
A Brief Memoir

I AM STEPPING AWAY FROM THE OVERVIEW of the Company to write my own brief memoir. Like many others, I have always loved to dance. My surgeon father thought dance lessons would be the thing to strengthen my lungs against my tendency to bronchitis. Little did he know that I would come to love dancing with a passion.

I had seen the Sadler's Wells Ballet (later the Royal Ballet) at the Royal Alexandra Theatre. I was enchanted and knew then I wanted to be a dancer, although I would never have admitted it. I told anyone who asked that I wanted to be an occupational therapist. I then saw a performance of *Sleeping Beauty* by the Royal Ballet—this time at the Maple Leaf Gardens. I was again enchanted and inspired. Much later, I saw Ulanova dance Juliet and thought she was the best in the world. That is what I wanted to be! The best.

I took my first lessons at ten years of age with Jean Macpherson in Ketchum Hall (now Jesse Ketchum School) on Davenport Road. It was called "Greek dancing." We danced in robin's egg-blue tunics and matching underpants, pink tights, and shoes. After a year, Jean Macpherson disappeared and long-legged Betty Oliphant, newly arrived from England, began to teach ballet lessons. I'll never forget Veronica Tennant and I arriving breathless from Bishop Strachan School to join the class in our middies, navy bloomers, and navy knee socks. I remember Betty, with her light grey eyes, standing at the barre and exclaiming, "Stand like a princess." And I did my best, middy and bloomers be damned!

Joceyln Terell in Winter Night.
Courtesy of the National Ballet Archives.

Betty had a semi-detached house on Sherbourne Street, south of Wellesley; she lived upstairs with her two daughters, Gail and Carol, and others. There were two studios on the main floor for teaching. For years I went to the Sherbourne Street studio every evening. At the time these studios seemed grand and spacious, but compared to the National Ballet School studios we would have in the future, these studios were small.

Finally, when I was in high school, Branksome Hall let me drop physics, math, and calculus, in order to have more time and energy for ballet classes. I thought it was very enlightened of the principal, Miss Reid, who was in her eighties. She did the same for another Branksome student, Wendy Griner, a serious skating student at the time.

I went into the Company at sixteen years of age, out of grade twelve, to replace Pauline McCullagh, who had broken her foot. This was much against my father's "better judgment" who thought I should first finish high school. I, frankly, was thrilled. I went to the beloved St. Lawrence Hall, the home of the National Ballet, where I had attended my summer schools. I joined the Company that year, 1956, in time for a summer engagement at the Carter-Barron Amphitheatre in Washington, DC. The Amphitheatre was in a park in the open air, on a stage backed by the Dancing Waters. I was now under the tutelage of Celia Franca, artistic director. I worshipped the ground she walked on. We youngsters would have done anything for her. I cut my teeth during the Carter-Barron engagement dancing Tudor's *Gala Performance, Les Sylphides,* and performing as a debutante in *Offenbach in the Underworld* (all the time wanting to do the can-can). Angela Leigh danced the Prelude in *Les Sylphides* beautifully, but had a black hanger caught on her wings. To add insult to injury, a little dog ran onstage during *Les Sylphides* (a ballet with predominantly white costumes and white scenery) and zigzagged across the stage, sniffing at the *corps de ballet,* before it was pulled into the wings by a stagehand. We couldn't help but burst out laughing at its antics, despite knowing we would hear about it in "corrections" from Miss Franca—and we did! On another occasion, Mrs. Nixon, wife of then U.S. President Nixon, and her two daughters came backstage for autographs

Earl Kraul, Patrick Hurde, and Jocelyn Terell, Fisherman and His Soul.
Courtesy: Private collection.

and we were honoured. At the top of the dented wooden stairs in St. Lawrence Hall was the famous bulletin board where all the casting for the upcoming season was posted. In my second year I read the bulletin board with mixed feelings. I was made a first soloist, despite my unfinished training with Betty Oliphant and my feeling that I had a weak technique. On the one hand, I was thrilled that Miss Franca had faith in me, casting me in new solo roles. On the other hand, I was absolutely terrified. *How could I possibly do these?* I wondered. I also felt sad that I could no longer be with my friends in the *corps de ballet* dressing room,

Patrick Hurde, Hans Meister, and Jocelyn Terell, One in Five.
Courtesy: Private collection.

but would have to move to the soloists' dressing room. Sounded a bit lonely. *Price of success,* I thought.

I performed the Waltz in *Les Sylphides.* Celia, who was generally known as a "monster lady," turned out to be a wonderful coach for me. She was tender and helpful to a young, green soloist, and infinitely patient. I was deeply touched by her coaching, although I never knew how to talk to her outside of rehearsals. It took me a while to figure out that Miss Franca was short of small talk herself. But she was able to turn very inexperienced dancers into fine interpreters of roles they weren't yet ready for. Being my

131

own worst critic, I have always been grateful for Miss Franca's encouraging coaching.

As we had a short season and were laid off from June to September, some of us danced on television and in the Canadian National Exhibition Grandstand Show, and some of us studied further, hoping to improve substandard technique. I, thanks to support from my family, went to New York City, where I studied with Margaret Craske and Antony Tudor backstage at the Metropolitan Opera ballet school. I loved studying with Craske, who taught Cecchetti, but most of all I was challenged by Tudor's classes, where he had a marvellous accompanist who improvised according to Tudor's *enchaînements* (a series of practice steps put together to make a short dance phrase). He put together very "dancey" combinations. He taught a tough class, and one always hoped to avoid being a target of his sarcastic wit. I found him kind and helpful. Perhaps he sensed my fear.

In the summer of 1959, I went to London, England, where I studied both with Miss Franca's favourite teach, Idzikowski, and with Audrey de Vos. One day, I took a class with Kathleen Crofton, the famous English dancer and teacher. Arnold Spohr of the Royal Winnipeg Ballet was watching and offered me a job! Though flattered, I returned to the National Ballet.

In 1962, after an ankle injury, I went to Kiev, thanks to my family, with Galina Samsova, a brilliant and strong Ukrainian dancer who was dancing with our Company at the time. I studied with Galina's teacher from St. Petersburg, Verekundova, and found that fractured French was indeed the international language of ballet. It got me through the classes she taught backstage at the Kiev Opera House. I found it very hard to measure myself against Ukrainian dancers who had been handpicked and had trained every day for ten years. Perhaps I was not going to be the best dancer in the world after all.

Betty Oliphant and Celia Franca were not very keen on our studying anywhere other than under their watchful eyes. They disagreed with my father's theory that young doctors needed to go abroad to finish their education, and that therefore young dancers needed to do the same. The comparison was not always apt.

I came home in 1962 and appeared again with the Company, especially in *One in Five,* a short, comic ballet that was a refreshing change from all the serious ballets I had appeared in.

I must say that my main partner, Earl Kraul, made a deep impression on me. His immense musicality and infinite patience with a green and often quaking Jocelyn touched me profoundly. I had other partners—Hans Meister and Donald Mahler in *Death and the Maiden* and Robert England in *Offenbach in the Underworld*—and learned something from all of them, but my heart went out to Earl.

As I write this, it is August of 2018, and the great humidity currently enveloping Toronto reminds me of dancing with the National Ballet in Florida in similar conditions. Makeup would run down our faces in sweaty rivulets, pointe shoes would go mushy in no time, and while I was happy to get my muscles warmed up more easily, I hated the heat. When we went swimming to escape it, we ended up with sunburns, and Celia Franca scolded us. "Professional dancers never get sunburned. You'd better apply wet white thickly for *Swan Lake.* You look more like flamingos than swans!" To me, there was something depressing about the heat and the grey-green Spanish moss hanging parasitically from the trees. Somehow, down south, nothing every dried out, and I felt permanently unsettled.

In contrast, when we danced in Northern Ontario or Quebec, we were always cold. We would wear hockey stockings and sweaters over our practice clothes or our costumes in the wings, reminding each other, "Hey, don't forget to take off your hockey stockings before you go on!" This cold was particularly penetrating when we danced in hockey arenas, where a plywood stage would have been built for us. We would warm up before the show in a class onstage and it would take forever to warm up my feet. Still, I preferred this cold to the humidity of Florida. Though it had its own challenges, I felt exhilarated, not depressed by the cold weather.

Thinking of mushy pointe shoes, I am reminded of the first time I ever bought pointe shoes from Bernadette Carpenter's shop on Yonge Street, near Charles, above an interesting jewellery shop. I went with my mother to buy my first pink satin pointe shoes. I had spent the first three years of my training in soft pink leather ballet slippers. Now my feet and legs were strengthened enough to start working *en pointe*—the long-awaited moment. We climbed the sagging wooden stairs to the third floor. My heart thudded from excitement as much as from the climb.

This was Bernadette Carpenter's, the dance supplies store where I had come to buy my soft ballet slippers, as well as pink Danskin tights and black leotards. This was the holy of holies for me, for every ballet student in Toronto, and for miles around. The small store had old wooden floors with narrow planks, a musty, dusty smell, and many coloured leotards hanging from the ceiling, wired into unlikely dance positions. I had been trained to look disdainfully at the pink puckered leotards with little tulle tutu skirts sewn onto them, or the sequin-decorated gauzy wings to wear at a spring recital. I knew that serious students stuck to the classical pink tights and dark leotard, with hair severely secured in a hairnet or pulled back in a bun, so that hair would not interfere with pirouettes or other movements. I followed these strictures without question. It was all part of becoming a dancer. Bernadette herself came forward to wait on us, and my mother explained that I needed to be fitted with my first pointe shoes. My mother was embarrassing. Why did she need to say that they were my *first* pointe shoes? I was already aware that I was the oldest in my class and rather late getting onto pointe. Bernadette was a greying, knowing sort of woman in a dark skirt over black tights, and a dark turtleneck sweater. She measured both of my feet with the same foot measure that any shoe store uses, and muttered to herself about Freed shoes, then went behind a dark grey curtain where the point shoes were stored. She came out a few minutes later with several ordinary-looking shoeboxes.

Bernadette explained what I already knew: there were three brands of pointe shoes to choose from—Frederick Freed of London, Gambas made in Italy, and Johnny Brown made in the U.S. She thought Freeds would fit me best. Gambas were for wide feet, and Johnny Browns are best for people without much arch. She pulled a pair of Freeds out of the tissue paper and I tried them on. They felt hard, tight, and uncomfortable. There was a small barre handy on the wall near the curtain, and she indicated

I should go over to it to try standing on pointe, supported. I held my breath and went up on both pointes. There was a mirror foot level, and I saw that I had "good" feet for pointe work—the requisite high arch that we students all prayed for. I tried to ignore the pinched feeling my feet had inside those hard-blocked toes, and Bernadette remarked kindly that they would soften up as I wore them and that I could use lambswool to protect my toes.

She suggested I try some other makes and sizes to make sure I had the best fit, but I ended up choosing the first pair I tried on—the Freed pointe shoes made in London, England. We then bought the pink ribbons to sew onto the pointe shoes that criss-crossed around my ankle and tied on the inside, with the ends tucked out of sight. This ribbon was grosgrain on the inside, and shiny satin on the outside. Ribbons had to be sewn on every pair, as well as a heel elastic that looped around the lower ankle to keep the heel of the shoes firmly in place. Then we bought heavy pink cotton thread, used to darn the toes of the shoes to prevent slipping and to hold the powdered resin that gave a further grip on any floor. I had to learn to darn my own pointe shoes, and my first pair would be etched with tiny stitches and much painstaking labour. Later, the stitches got larger and further apart.

Eventually I had to buy vamp elastic. This was elastic about two inches wide, made for students who had such a high arch that they needed extra support across the front of the arch until they could strengthen the foot muscles. Such a high arch was the envy of the stockier students with lower arched feet, but it took a long time for these beautiful feet to become strong *en pointe*. My mother, almost as excited as I, took the bag and handed it to me. We said goodbye to Bernadette and clambered down the wooden stairs, out into the sunlight once again.

I took that first pair of pointe shoes home almost reverently and spent hours sewing on the shiny pink ribbons and the pink heel elastics, and darning those toes like a work of art. I soon learned from the other students to break in the hard toes of the pointe shoes by putting them in the crack of the door next to the hinges and closing the door on them. *Crack!* You had to do it with just the right amount of pressure—too much and you would damage the shoes, too little and they would stay in their pristine glue-hardened state. I also quickly learned to hold the heels of the pointe shoes (*never* "toe" shoes) under cold tap water to saturate them so that they would not slip off the heel. Failing water, I would use my own spit. Spit or water also worked to make sure the ends of the ribbons stayed tucked in around the ankles.

I bought boxes of lambswool at the dance supply store to cushion my toes in a wad of lambswool every time I put the pointe shoes on. This did not always prevent nasty, painful blisters from forming, and we trained ourselves to put rubbing alcohol on them at night to dry them up quickly. This hurt, and we blew furiously on the alcohol-drenched blister to lessen the burning. After a while, callouses developed on our toes and blistering occurred less frequently. Our bare feet, calloused and bunioned, looked terrible with a bikini, but of course that was all part of the price we acolytes gladly paid.

We were aware of the existence of "toe caps" to cushion toes in place of lambswool, but were disdainful of them. Lambswool was the choice of *professionals,* and we somehow associated those leather, furry toe caps with sequined recitals and rhinestone earrings and all things tasteless, vulgar, and simple in the ballet world. Strait is the gait, I suppose. Later we discovered a style of pointe shoes in the U.S. that came with a suede toe that the wearer wouldn't have to darn themselves. But I never tried them, though, and was, like the rest of my peers, rather disdainful about them as well. We were insufferable little purists!

Upon my entry into the National Ballet Company as a green sixteen-year-old, I soon learned the unique fashions of the ballet world that I hadn't known while still a student. The girls wore all kinds of elaborate garb over their basic pink tights and black leotards, and the boys wore black tights and white T-shirts. This fashion, I was to discover, was partly for fun and frivolity, but partly to meet other needs.

Most of the dancers wore knitted legwarmers to keep their muscles warm, especially in rehearsals that could be very stop-and-go. These legwarmers were usually knitted hockey stockings—the bright blue and white of the Maple Leafs, or the lurid red of the Canadiens. Once in an outdoor amphitheatre, a principal dancer went onstage in the white romantic ballet,

Les Sylphides, wearing her red Canadiens hockey stockings and ruined the romantic mood. I relied on the legwarmers myself to help warm up my perpetually cold feet. Girls often wore a short cardigan sweater and tied it at the front to shore up their often scanty breasts, and to leave the waist clear for partnering. I learned, too, that in rehearsals for certain ballets the principal girls often wore a flimsy split skirt to simulate a costume, but also to feel swishy and swirly.

I feared injury, as all dancers do. An injury meant getting laid off to heal while another dancer took over hard-won roles. At worst, an injury could finish your career—a short career to begin with, as most dancers are finished by forty. I always felt as though I were in a race against time, and like most dancers, feared injury as a fate worse than death. To help prevent injuries, we would sometimes opt to wear leather knee or elbow pads during rehearsals of strenuous modern ballets. A dancer with a bad knee might wear an elastic bandage around it. Thus, a dancer's garb, which could seem strange to an outsider's eye, was partly a superstitious talisman against injuries.

Dancers spend much of their time gazing into a mirror. They are acutely aware of their own bodies and don garments to hide what they consider to be unpalatable body parts. Teachers and artistic directors could constantly allude to a dancer's weight or the size of her various "assets." I saw many a dancer shrivel from this kind of comment. Sometimes a dancer might resort to wrapping plastic around a body part, such as a thigh, with the hopes that encouraging the extra sweating would speed up weight loss. Behind the scenes, ballet was not for the faint of heart.

Many dancers like myself start training at a young age and want only to dance. There are never enough jobs and so a teacher or artistic director's words could make or break a dancer's chance at a career. Like my colleagues, I became utterly dependent upon a good word from those in power. Praise set me up. Adverse criticism cast me down to the depths. Worst yet was the silent treatment, when I could only imagine that my performance did not even merit a comment.

Internationally, the dance world is a punitive culture, and that seems unlikely to change. In a deeply competitive and authority-oriented world, our dance fashions consoled us. We found some sense of independence in the garments we put on our bodies. It was, I suppose, a token defiance of the norm.

Yet, all of the training and fashions did not prepare me for the injury that would end my dance career. I danced into 1964, when I injured my back. A year later, fed up with being sidelined by so many injuries, I made the painful decision to give up ballet as a career. Upon my leaving, I felt like a moth coming out of a chrysalis—vulnerable and ill-equipped for life. Dance fashions no longer helped.

Tearfully, I made the decision to go to Shaw's to learn to type. In the fall of 1965, I went to York University as a "mature" student. Though life had seemed to fall to ashes, it turned out that I loved attending classes at York where I studied English and History. It was a brave new world for me. In 1981, I went on to complete a Masters degree at the University of Toronto, and studied Freefall writing with Barbara Turner-Vesselago. In between these degrees, I married Peter Allen in 1968 and had three sons, Eric, Geoff, and Christopher. I now have six grandchildren.

I sat on the board of both the National Ballet School and Peggy Baker Dance Projects. I taught a little but found it very difficult to be so near and yet so far from performing. It is no surprise to miss dancing—my identity became wrapped up with ballet very early in my life. The years dancing with the National Ballet of Canada were among the most challenging and happiest of my life. I loved performing and was always "fed" by the audience. It was a crucial exchange.

Who knew that late in life I would also be struck by a rare neurological illness—progressive, supranuclear palsy—that would affect my balance (woe for an ex-dancer) and my speech. There are always surprises in life. I have learned to be satisfied in many areas at once instead of having one all-encompassing calling, but I often still miss that calling.

10.
Afterword

IF EVER WE NEEDED PROOF that the founding of our National Ballet of Canada was a collective miracle, it is in hearing afresh (and often anew) the voices of courage, individuality and vibrancy of those dancers from the fearless fifties. So pure, so brave, so resonant. I find it enthralling and deeply moving to have their personal stories re-awakened, and to collect a panoply of memories that are seminal to us all.

First, I must salute Jocelyn Terell for this massive undertaking—truly her passion project. Too many of our early heroes have left us, and her conviction that this compelling memoir must be recorded offers us a most important sequence of Canadian dance history. As a ballet child of the late 1950s (one of Betty Oliphant's Sherbourne Street students), I remember how Miss O. would hold Jocey up to us as an example of balletic lyricism and beauty—coming from Miss O. that was really something! Betty's own signature gift for all who were trained by her—and her part in the formation of our Canadian balletic style—was the fluidity of her *port-de-bras* and that very special quality of lyricism. She would enjoin us to watch Jocey closely and we—albeit from that top balcony of the Royal Alexandra Theatre—remember her poignant performances in *Winter Night, Lilac Garden* and *Death and the Maiden* vividly. She was a beautiful dancer!

Our formative training years with Miss O. were characterized by her demands for technique, quality, and classicism; our skills were then honed and refined by Miss Franca with her consummate artistry, musicality, and professionalism.

At summer school, from the elevated platform of the majestically dilapidated St. Lawrence Hall, we avidly watched the Company class and rehearsals, conducted with precision and panache by the charismatic Celia. And even if we, at age nine, could not then fathom the extent of the sacrifices these bold young dancers were making, we did indeed absorb and retain every second of an experience we recognized as precious. They were blazing trails for us—the next generation—for the privilege of a full education, a fully-formed ballet company structure, and a developing public appreciation of ballet as a profession in Canada.

What is critical to remember about *Early Days, Early Dancers*, is that far from being a sentimental collection of memories (one of Celia's most caustic corrections delivered with an expression of disgust was "too sentimental, darling"), it traces the imprint of an era. What resounds from these personal pages is the indelible impact that Celia Franca and Betty Oliphant made on Canadian ballet. They trained us in communal effort, group striving, and shared pride. Such standards, discipline, taste, and style—these are the legacies that are emblematic of the National Ballet of Canada to this day.

More than any other art form, I think classical ballet and dance has evolved on an historical continuum, a connected chain of common experience, from generation to generation that has lived for centuries. From that very first lesson to the very last day of one's dancing life—whether ten or fifty years later—it always begins at the barre. This unique continuity physically links each dancer to the next, every single day in first position, placing hands on the barre: handing it on—passing it on—persevering.

As Celia said to me, in the closing line of *The Dancers' Story*, celebrating the National Ballet's fiftieth anniversary, broadcast on CBC in 2001: "The Dancers' Story? Why, without the Dancers, of course we couldn't do anything. I don't quite know how to thank all those people"

> —Veronica Tennant, C.C., Filmmaker, Writer, Principal Dancer, The National Ballet of Canada, 1964 to 1989.

Bibliography.

Bell, Kenneth. *The National Ballet of Canada: A Celebration.* Toronto: University of Toronto Press, 1978.

Bishop-Gwyn, Carol. *The Pursuit of Perfection: A Life of Celia Franca.* Toronto: Cormorant Books, 2011.

Brockhouse, Robert. *Royal Alexander Theatre: A Celebration of 100 Years.* Toronto: McArthur & Co., 2008.

Campbell, Norman, dir. *Swan Lake.* CBC, 1956.

Fisher-Stitt, Norma Sue. *The Ballet Class: A History of Canada's National Ballet School, 1959-2009.* Toronto: National Ballet School, 2010.

Franca, Celia. "Television Specials Canada and England." *Balletopics: The National Ballet of Canada Magazine* 8.4 (October 1968): 7.

Morrison, Simon. "Meet Boris Volkoff, 'the father of Canadian ballet.'" *The Globe and Mail* 11 October 2016. Web.

Neufeld, James. *Passion to Dance: The National Ballet of Canada.* Toronto: Dundurn Press, 2011.

Tennant, Veronica, dir. *The Dancer's Story: The National Ballet of Canada.* Documentary, Sound Venture Productions, 2002.

Tennant, Veronica, dir. *Celia Franca: Tour de Force.* Documentary, Sound Venture Productions, 2006.

Tribute Contributors

Meredith Adams received a Bachelor of Education degree from the University of Alberta in 1977 and began teaching in northern Alberta. In 1980/81, she studied musical theatre at Grant MacEwan College in Edmonton, where she took dance classes from David Adams. During this time, she also completed the requirements for an Associate Diploma, one of two highest standings awarded ARCT (Piano Teacher) diploma from the Royal Conservatory of Music. In the 1980s, she did some performing and taught early childhood music classes with Alberta College, eventually settling on a fulfilling career as a private piano instructor. In 2008, Meredith, along with Janine Adams (David Adams's daughter with Lois Smith) and Gunnar Blodgett (one of David's former students), completed a research project on the Life and Legacy of David Adams, funded by the Alberta Foundation for the Arts.

Dance artist and author **Carol Anderson** has chronicled Canadian dance since the 1980s. She has performed, choreographed, and taught in numerous professional, educational and community settings since the 1970s. Professor Emerita of York University's Department of Dance, Anderson continues to write, move, teach, and create.

Peggy Baker is one of Canada's most celebrated and influential dance artists, respected as a performer in the work of esteemed Canadian and American creators; as an educator in important dance programs throughout North America; and as a choreographer of poetic and visually striking works for her Toronto based company, Peggy Baker Dance Projects. Artist-in-Residence at Canada's National Ballet School, Ms. Baker's many honours include the Order of Canada, the Governor General's Award, the Premier's Award, the Carsen Prize, Honorary Doctorates from York and the University of Calgary, a 2017 Bogliasco Foundation fellowship, and six Doras.

Cheryl Belkin Epstein is the Developer of Creative Resources and Ballet Historian at Canada's National Ballet School. In this capacity, her responsibilities include teaching the History of Dance in both the Professional Ballet and Teacher Training Programs and co-coordinating Career Planning for the senior students. Belkin Epstein trained in ballet in Winnipeg and danced with Winnipeg's Contemporary Dancers and *Les Feux-Follets* of Montréal. On retiring from dance, she returned to school and was called to the Ontario Bar in 1981. She practised corporate law at McCarthy & McCarthy in Toronto until 1983 and later, while living abroad for many years, worked in the Legal Department of the Bank of Israel and did freelance legal editing and writing in Morocco and France. Returning to Canada, she began the study of dance history; first at the National Ballet School and later at York University where she obtained an MA in Dance History. Over the years, she has served on a number of arts boards. She currently serves on the Board of Directors of Peggy Baker Dance Projects.

Judie Colpman (aka Nora Brown) is a Charter Member of The National Ballet of Canada (1952 to 1962). Ms. Colpman has performed as a dancer, actor, and currently works as a director, choreographer, and playwright in Canada, the United States, and Europe.

Michael Crabb is a Toronto-based arts journalist, broadcaster, and lecturer and has written about dance internationally for almost forty years. He was a CBC Radio producer and on-air host from 1981 through 2000. He is currently dance critic for *The Toronto Star*.

John Fraser is the former dance and theatre critic for *The Globe and Mail* and was also that newspaper's correspondent in Beijing and, later, in London. He was editor of *Saturday Night* magazine for seven years and then went on to be Master of Massey College in the University of Toronto for two decades. Currently, he is Executive Chair of the National NewsMedia Council of Canada.

Vanessa Harwood was born in England, and raised in Toronto, attending the National Ballet School as an original student in 1959, graduating in 1964. She joined the National Ballet of Canada in 1965 and became a principal dancer in 1970 until leaving the company in 1987. She coached bronze medal 1988 World and Olympic Ice Dance Champions, Tracy Wilson and Robert McCall. In 1989, she made her acting debut with the Kingston Grand Theatre as Mollie Ralston in *The Mousetrap* in 1989. In 1991, Harwood also appeared as the ballerina in the film *Stepping Out*, starring Liza Minelli. She spent a season as Artistic Associate with Theatre Plus Toronto. She has also appeared on the televisions shows *Road to Avonlea*, *Due South*, and *Nero Wolfe*. Ms. Harwood was Artistic Director of Balletto Classico from 1989 to 1993. She was honoured as an Officer of the Order of Canada in 1984. She received the Queen's Silver Jubilee Medal 1992, Queen's Golden Jubilee Medal 2002, and Queen's Diamond Jubilee Medal in 2012. She has been a photographer for the last twenty years, using her images for a line of greeting cards for all occasions. She has also exhibited at a number of galleries and shows including the National Ballet Art Show at the Sony Centre.

Lilian Jarvis was one of the inaugural dancers of the National Ballet from its official beginning official opening in 1951 until 1963 when she left to study in New York City. Known for her lyrical and musical qualities, Lilian was famous for her lead role in Celia Franca's *L'après midi d'un faun*, one of her own favourite roles to dance. Lilian's other roles ranged from Giselle in the "white" ballets to the Tudor ballets *Serenade* and *Lilac Garden*, and the character roles of *Coppelia* and *Pineapple Poll*, as well as Debutante in *Offenbach in the Underworld*. Lilian made dance history when she came out of a twelve-year retirement at the age of forty-five to dance the role of Juliet at the National Ballet's twenty-fifth anniversary performance of *Romeo and Juliet* for the first and only time. Lilian left the company in 1963 to further her ballet studies in New York City and subsequently became enthralled with the Martha Graham modern dance technique. From there, her career took a major turn when, beginning in the late seventies, she created her own Graham-based teaching method, currently known as "Somatic Stretch: The Jarvis Technique." Lilian continues to teach her method both in class and online alongside her daughter, Meredith Sands Keator.

Selma Landen Odom is a dance historian and writer. Recruited to York University in 1972, she was founding director of the Masters and Ph.D. programs in Dance and Dance Studies, the first offered of their kind in Canada. Professor Emerita at York, she is also an Adjunct of the Centre for Drama, Theatre and Performance Studies of at the University of Toronto. With a practical dance background and degrees in English literature, History of Theatre, and Dance Studies, she has published articles and reviews since the 1960s. She has contributed to scholarly and professional conferences and organizations, curated exhibitions and film festivals, advised publishers and consulted for various cultural agencies. For many years, she served on the Board of Directors of for Dance Collection Danse, Canada's national dance archive and museum. She co-edited the anthology *Canadian Dance: Visions and Stories* (2004) and co-authored *Practical Idealists: Founders of the London School of Dalcroze Eurhythmics* (2013). Her continuing research focuses on the sources, practices, and influences of the Dalcroze method of music and movement education.

Myriam Guevara Mann is director of Escuela de Danzas Teresa Mann, a dance school in Panama City founded by her mother. Born in Panama, she moved to Toronto at twenty-one years old and worked as a professional dancer from 1988 to 2000. She then returned to Panama to take over as director of her mother's school. She and her students have performed in world-class competitions and shows all over the globe, and as featured performers at World Youth Day.

Annette av Paul was born in Sweden in 1944 and accepted into the Royal Swedish Ballet school at the age of eight. At seventeen, she was picked by choreographer Yuri Grigorovich (later the director of the Bolshoi Ballet) to dance the principal role of Katerina in his full-length ballet, *The Stone Flower*. In 1964, she married Canadian choreographer, Brian Macdonald, who brought her to Canada. After a successful performing career, Annette took on teaching roles at the National Ballet of Canada and the National Ballet School, among others, and has served on the board of many ballet companies, including Ballet British Columbia in its inception. Annette and Brian lived in Montreal until they settled in Stratford, Ontario, in 1985, where both became involved in many creative capacities in the Stratford Festival.

Joysanne Sidimus, M.SM., was born in New York and trained with George Balanchine. She was a dancer with the New York City Ballet and went on to become a principal dancer with the National Ballet of Canada and the Pennsylvania Ballet. After retiring from performing, she taught and staged Balanchine works for fifteen years and founded the Dancer Transition Resource Centre, serving as its executive director until December 2005. She was also the founding vice-chair of Toronto Western Hospital's Artists' Health Centre and became the project director for the Senior Artists' Research Project. She continues to work as a Balanchine *répétiteur* for the Balanchine Trust both in Canada and internationally. She is the recipient of both the Governor General's Meritorious Service Medal and the 2006 Governor General's Performing Arts Award for Lifetime Artistic Achievement.

Timothy Spain appeared at age thirteen as the child, Orestes, in the National Ballet of Canada's *House of Atreus*, the same production in which Earl Kraul played Orestes as an adult. In 1968, he joined the National Ballet as a full-time member and danced with them until 1972. Later, he performed with London's

Festival Ballet, the Molly Molloy Dance Theatre, and freelanced in London, Paris, and other European centres. He choreographed for the National Ballet of Canada, London's Festival Ballet, and for television and commercial productions in England, Canada, and France. In 2004, he joined Toronto's Bishop Strachan School, where he continues to teach on a part-time basis.

Mavis Staines is a former dancer with the National Ballet of Canada and current Artistic Director of the National Ballet School.

Veronica Tennant, C.C., spent her illustrious twenty-five-year career as Prima Ballerina with The National Ballet of Canada. She won a devoted following on the international stage as a dancer of extraordinary versatility and dramatic power. Born in London, England, Veronica Tennant began her ballet lessons at the age of four with the Arts Educational School. Upon moving to Canada at the age of nine, Veronica started training with Betty Oliphant and then the National Ballet School. While she missed a year of training due to her first back injury, she entered the National Ballet Company in 1964 as its youngest principal dancer, chosen by Celia Franca and John Cranko for her debut as *Juliet*. She went on to earn accolades in every major classical role and extensive neo-classical repertoire as well as having several contemporary ballets choreographed for her. She worked with the legendary choreographers Sir Frederick Ashton, Roland Petit, Jiří Kylián, John Neumeier, and championed Canadian choreographers such as James Kudelka, Ann Ditchburn, Constantin Patsalas, and David Allan. Tennant is now an established and multi award-winning filmmaker, producer, and director. She was the first dancer in Canada to be made an Officer of the Order of Canada in 1975 and in 2003 was elevated to the rank of Companion of the Order of Canada, the Order's highest honour.

Acknowledgements

I want to thank two people for first giving me the idea for this book: Oldyna Dynowska, charter member of the company; and Cheryl Belkin-Epstein, who teaches History of Ballet at the National Ballet School and is a former dancer herself.

I am most grateful to Karen Kain, until recently Artistic Director of the National Ballet Company and former ballerina, who wrote the foreword and opened the National Ballet Archives to me. This work is my way of celebrating the anniversary of her association with the National Ballet Company.

I also want to thank Veronica Tennant, another former ballerina and current film director, who wrote the afterword, the tribute to Janet and David Scott, plus the wonderful tribute to Earl Kraul. She offered all kinds of encouragement and gave me access to her film, The Dancers' Story.

Thank you to Luciana Ricciutelli, a wonderful editor, and Inanna Publications for publishing this book.

A special thank you to my long-time friend and colleague, Dr. Marion Lynn.

Many thanks to Mavis Staines, Artistic Director of Canada's National Ballet School, who wrote the tribute to Glenn Gilmour, and who was always very kind and encouraging regarding this book.

I also want to thank Barbara Turner-Vesselago for her inspiring creative writing workshops. I am also grateful to my writing group Anna Van Straubenzee, Fran Turner, Marie Laurin, Andrew Ignatieff, for their honest and critical responses.

I want to thank Tiffany Maxwell, my assistant editor and speedy typist without whom this book would not have been written.

I want to acknowledge the skill and organizational wizardry of my assistant, Patricia Maxwell. Her help made all the difference in finishing this book.

I want to thank Ilda Labao and Marc McNamara who worked tirelessly to ensure that I had the quiet to work on the book.

I want to thank my sons Eric, Geoff, Chris, and my sister, Daphne Payne, who were always supportive.

As for Bob Ito, Donald Mahler, Edelayne Brandt, Frances Greenwood, Gloria Bonnell, Janet Green Foster, Judie Colpman, Katerina Evanova, Lilian Jarvis, Marcel Chojnacki, Myrna Aaron, Oldyna Dynowska, Pauline McCullagh, Penny Anne Winter, Sally Brayley Bliss, Shirley Kash, Valerie Lyon, Vicky Bertram, Yves Cousineau, Lorna Geddes, Cathy Carr, Cecily Paige, Marilyn Rollo, and Leila Zorina: they, above all, deserve my gratitude and praise.

Another group of people I wish to express my great appreciation and thanks to are those who wrote memorial tributes in the "Early Champions" chapter about those from the fifties who have died.

National Ballet Company archivists Adrienne Neville, Caitlin Dyer, and especially Katherine Wilson, were all most helpful to the book.

Dance Collection Danse's Miriam Adams and Amy Bowring gave me early photos and much moral support.

Photo: Nicholas Wong

Jocelyn Terell Allen became a dancer with the National Ballet Company in 1956, at the age of sixteen. She danced for the first time, as a member of the *corps de ballet*, in the Carter-Barron Amphitheatre in Washington, DC, studied dance in New York and London as a member of the Company, and became a principal dancer in the fall of 1963. She danced for half her life and then a series of injuries forced her to have to adjust to life without dance. She enrolled in York University as a "mature" student and subsequently completed a Master's degree in English at the University of Toronto. In later years, she was privileged to sit on the boards of the Dancer Transition Resource Centre, or DTRC, and Peggy Baker Dance Projects. She married Peter Allen, had three sons, and now has six grandchildren. She continues to enjoy attending ballet, theatre, and the arts, and she loves to write.